LIGHTYEAR

~~IT'S WHAT YOU DO WITH THOSE THOUGHTS~~

~~THAT DETERMINES IF YOU'RE A LOST CAUSE OR NOT~~

LIGHTYEAR

~~JUST CAUSE YOU'RE FLOATING AROUND IN SPACE~~

~~DOESN'T MAKE YOU AN ASTRONAUT~~

JOSHUA HORGOS

gatekeeper press™

Tampa, Florida

Lightyear

Published by Gatekeeper Press
7853 Gunn Hwy, Suite 209
Tampa, FL 33626
www.GatekeeperPress.com

ISBN (paperback): 9781662926815
eISBN: 9781662926822

Library of Congress Catalog Card Number: 2022946025

For the Broken & Hurting

TABLE OF CONTENTS

My prayer is that the Holy Spirit will wrestle with you
through the pages of this book and
remove the veil from your heart so that you may be
"transformed into His image with ever increasing glory
[which comes from the Lord, who is the Spirit]."

II Corinthians 3:18

INTRODUCTION

MY NAME IS JOSH. IT'S NICE TA MEET'CHA.
I CLIMBED UP OUT OF THE GUTTER SO THESE WORDS MIGHT REACH YA.
FUNDAMENTALLY AWKWARD AT FIRST,
BUT I'LL ADMIT,
I WAS CREATED FROM WORDS & A HANDFUL OF DIRT.
YOU CAN CHOP UP THAT LAST LINE & PUT IT IN YOUR NOSTRIL,
THE "BREATH OF LIFE" CAME & TRANSFORMED INTO THE GOSPEL.

THIS LITERARY FEATURE IS AN OBEDIENT PROCEDURE,
SHARING MY TRIALS & TRIBULATIONS AS AN ON 'N OFF BELIEVER.
RELATABLE NAVIGATION THRU DAILY DELIBERATION,
COMFORTING THE TORMENT WITH CHRISTIAN CONVERSATION.
ALLOWING THE SOUL TO BREATHE UNDER THE PRESSURES OF
THIS EARTH,
SEEKING RELIEF, FINDING PEACE, GAINING VALUE & SELF—WORTH.

WE ALL GOT OUR QUESTIONS;
MAYBE YOU'LL FIND SOME ANSWERS HERE...
THIS IS LIGHTYEAR.

JOHN 1:1

1 In the beginning was the Word, and the Word was with God,
and the Word was God.

GENESIS 2:7

7 Then the LORD God formed a man from the dust of the ground and breathed into
his nostrils the breath of life, and the man became a living being.

ROMANS 1:16-17

16 For I am not ashamed of the gospel, because it is the power of God that brings
salvation to everyone who believes... **17** For in the gospel the righteousness of
God is revealed...

HABAKKUK 2:4

"**4** ...The righteous person will live by his faithfulness..."

Welcome. Grab a pen and some paper. Write down your thoughts.
Write out some prayers. This is a workable manuscript, an interactive
study guide, a reference point. LIGHTYEAR is intended to deepen
your understanding of God and better understand yourself. No matter
what you are going through, you are not alone. It's okay to have
questions and doubts. It's okay to feel shame & guilt. It's okay to be
joyful, excited, and celebrate accomplishments!

This book encourages you to recognize your emotions, be open minded
about behavioral patterns, and live a more freeing life without the
bondage of sin.

Write down a few questions right now, a few goals, and pray about
them. What are you hoping to achieve with this study? What do you
want to learn? Ask God to reveal Himself to you and provide the
understanding and the wisdom you are searching for.

Learning and growing is a process.

Enjoy.

STUMBLED SOME

I KNOW I'VE STUMBLED SOME; THIS IS NOTHING NEW.
I'VE LIED, I'VE CHEATED, I'VE STOLEN TOO.
AT GUNPOINT, IN KNIFE FIGHTS,
COPS FLASHING LIGHTS & MISSING SHOES.
BEEN PUNK'D & JUMPED...RUN OVER ONCE.
BROKEN BONES, BROKEN HOMES, BLACK EYES BRUISED.
SIMPLY PUT, I'M BORN TO LOSE.
TROUBLED YOUTH, GANGSTER SCHOOL,
ADDICTED, ABUSED, MILITARY REFUSED.
REHAB, RELAPSE, COUNTY JAIL FOOD.
ALONE, DISTURBED, HURTING, CONFUSED.
HOMELESS, NO FOOD, NO DIRECTION, NO CLUE.

ENOUGH IS ENOUGH. MY WAY SUCKS.
THIS VICIOUS CYCLE, THIS CONSTANT BAD LUCK.
I KNOW THERE'S MORE.
SOMETHING BETTER THAN BEFORE.
REPENT, RESIST, MY WILL, NOW YOURS.
MY STRUGGLES, MY HARDSHIPS, MY HATRED, MY HURTS.
MY DENIAL, MY CURSE WORDS, MY VIOLENCE, PERVERSE.
BAD DECISIONS, POOR HEALTH, PLEASE... RID ME OF MYSELF!

MY PRAYERS, YOUR ANSWERS, YOUR PATH, MY FEET.
YOUR WORDS, MY TONGUE, MY MOUTH, YOU SPEAK.
CRYING, WHINING, TO YOU, FOR HELP.
SCREAMING, PLEADING, THIS DISTANCE, I'VE FELT.
THE CRIME, THE GRIND; THIS FOGGY MIND
HAS FINALLY REALIZED – YOU'VE BEEN HERE THE WHOLE TIME.

EZEKIEL 18:21–22, 30–32

21 "But if a wicked person turns away from all the sins they have committed… that person will surely live… **22** None of the offenses they have committed will be remembered…"
30 "…I will judge each of you according to your own ways…Repent! … **31** Rid yourselves of all the offenses you have committed, and get a new heart and a new spirit… **32** …Repent and live!"

1 PETER 5:10

10 And the God of all grace, who called you to his eternal glory in Christ, after you have suffered a little while, will himself restore you and make you strong, firm and steadfast.

EPHESIANS 4:31–32

31 Get rid of all bitterness, rage and anger, brawling and slander, along with every form of malice. **32** Be kind and compassionate to one another, forgiving each other, just as in Christ God forgave you.

ROMANS 8:28

28 … in all things God works for the good of those who love him, who have been called according to his purpose.

God loves us SO much; He is the one that gives us free will. We are free to make our own decisions. Believe it or not, even those who have wronged us are loved by God because He also created them and with the same free will. Unfortunately, our decisions, and the decisions of others, are often times not God's intentions and now we are stuck with the consequences and/or the pain of either being hurt or being the one that has done the hurting.

At some point we will need to repent, to turn away from our "wickedness," our "un-righteousness" and seek the forgiveness our Father in Heaven DESIRES to give us. We are also called to forgive those who have done wrong to us… Don't create an overwhelming list and set out going door to door, collecting checkmarks; rather, search the heart for un-wanted burdens and write out your requests and your grievances before God. Trust that He will handle them with love and guide you with assurance.

Regularly asking God for forgiveness is an obedient action of faith, and what a relief to know that He will forgive and wants to forgive so we're not walking around carrying the burden of sin that Jesus already died for. Asking God to forgive the same wrongdoings, over and over again eventually becomes embarrassing.

Can you identify repeat sin in your life? Are you getting sick of it? Embarrassed?

Where do you need/want forgiveness? Whom do you need/want to forgive? Besides Jesus, who can you open up to about this sin and ask for prayer in these areas?

Sometimes a little earthly accountability makes a big eternal difference.

IT'S COMPLICATED

IT'S COMPLICATED.
IT'S A BACK 'N FORTH, UP 'N DOWN, AGITATED WAIT.
IT'S AN IN 'N OUT, OVER UNDER, SEPARATED FATE.
IT'S A HOW COME, HOW MUCH, CAN WE REALLY TAKE?
A WHY NOT, SINCE WHEN, DO WE TOLERATE,
ALL THIS & THAT, TURBULENT BELLYACHE?

A PAINTED FACE, A TAINTED RACE,
AN EXPLOITED LIFE OF CHASING FAKE.
IT'S NOT AUTHENTIC, NOT CUSTOM MADE.
A PRE-PROGRAMMED VISION OF HOW WE'RE SUPPOSED TO BEHAVE.
THE DEEPER WE GO, THE MORE DENSE IT GETS.
TOTAL RELIANCE ON ARTIFICIAL INTELLIGENCE.
CAN'T THINK FOR YOURSELF; HERE WE GO AGAIN,
BELIEVE EVERYTHING THEY SAY,
ROBO-SAPIEN.

TEARS PUSH THE FOG FROM MY EYES & RINSE THE DIRT FROM
MY SOUL.
FOR A MOMENT I'M CURED; FOR A SECOND, I'M PURE.

I KNOW THERE'S A PLAN & IT'S YOURS, SO IT'S PERFECT!
HELP ME TO FLOAT AGAINST THIS CULTURAL CURRENT,
SPREADING YOUR LOVE, A PIVOTAL SERVANT,
EXTENDING A HAND TO THE BROKEN & HURTIN'.

ROMANS 12:2

2 Do not conform to the pattern of this world, but be transformed by the renewing of your mind. Then you will be able to test and approve what God's will is—his good, pleasing and perfect will.

ROMANS 5:3-4

3 ...because we know that suffering produces perseverance; 4 perseverance, character; and character, hope.

3 JOHN 1:11

11 Dear friend, do not imitate what is evil but what is good. Anyone who does what is good is from God. Anyone who does what is evil has not seen God.

PSALM 43:1

1 Vindicate me, my God, and plead my cause against an unfaithful nation. Rescue me from those who are deceitful and wicked.

Life can be a hard road to travel. Confusing. Un-certain. Mysterious even. Not knowing what you're "supposed" to be doing or saying can cause all types of anxieties and depressions. Society offers you the remedy in many forms, and all are available at your fingertips. "They" create the illusion of an easily, achievable, appealing life "IF...you do this, have this, take this, live like this..."

How is this "advertised" life going? Are you really satisfied, or is there still something missing?

LIGHTYEAR wants you to challenge yourself. Challenge your thoughts, your actions, your motives. Ask yourself "why?" Dig deeper into what makes you "tick" and what really motivates you to make a difference. Understand that God is a great resource for help, hope, and guidance. When you overcome challenges, you gain confidence and fulfillment; maybe even a better understanding of purpose.

What will you set out to accomplish next? How will this next accomplishment impact your life or the life of someone else? Think about it. Write it down. Create a plan. Highlight a few bullet points to help yourself stay on track and execute. You'll be glad you did.

I NEED HELP

I NEED HELP. I NEED A FAVOR;
THIS LOST SHEEP CAN'T KEEP UP. I NEED A SAVIOR.

NO MIRRORS, NO SMOKE, NO PALM-READING FOLKS.
NO LAMPS, NO GENIES, NO POTIONS TO CHOKE.
NO MAGIC, NO PILLS, NO CARDS CAN PROVOKE,
A FULLNESS WHEREIN, THIS VOID HAS ENTHRONED.

DISCOMFORT IS WIDE; THIS EMPTY SEARCH IS A BOTHER.
I REACH TOWARD THE SKY, FOR HELP FROM MY FATHER.

Oh, the avenues we explore, either publicly or in secret to answer our
questions and mask our insecurities... How temporary the results...
How great the need for repeat occurrence', developed tolerance...

Yet, here we have a loving, eternal Father, who wants to help us; whom
we instinctively cry out to during extreme moments of fear, pain,
excitement, even euphoria... "Oh my God..." There's no denying His
existence—instinct conquers reason.

Let's get God off the back burner and start giving Him first dibs at our
needs; especially since we know He exists. The very name of God is
hardwired right into our brains and the very cells of our bodies, the
parts we can't even explain.

BASIC INSTRUCTIONS BEFORE LEAVING EARTH

HEARTFELT. COURAGEOUS.
SMART HELP. CONTAGIOUS.
DEEP REITERATION OF LIFE'S STEALTH AGES.
A COMPILATION OF DISOBEDIENT PHASES.
VOLATILE, LATERAL, & OUTRAGEOUS!
AN EXCLAMATION OF DEVELOPING STAGES.
A HISTORY THAT PRE-DATES US,
YET DISRUPTS THE COMPLACENT WITH PROPHETIC STATEMENTS.

THIS IS LIFE CHANGING.
THE GREAT AWAKENING.
FORESHADOWING THE EPITOME OF HUMAN KIND, BREATHTAKING.
EARTHSHAKING.
DIABOLICAL SNAKING, REPTILIAN WAVERING.
REGRESSIVE APPROACH BACK-FIRED, NOW MIS-LABELING.
UN-VEILING...

TRUTH BE TOLD THRU SANDAL-TOED, DESERT-STROLLIN' YOUTH.
RIVER-DIPPIN', PRAISE-BE-GIVIN', MIRACLE-MAKIN' PROOF.
PAGES WRITTEN, EGYPTIAN VISION,
HEBREW BRAZEN SPEAK.
ARAMAIC, ANTIQUATED, LATIN TONGUE & GREEK.
METAPHORIC SYMBOLISM, LITERAL & DISCREET.
SLIGHTLY RHETORICAL VANTAGE POINT,
READING BETWEEN THE SHEETS.

COUNTLESS STORAGE OF ALIEN STORIES,
MESSENGERS OF FAITH.
MORALS, VALUES, SCAVENGERS,
TRIVIAL LIVES AT STAKE.
ASKING QUESTIONS, PRAYERS BE ANSWERED;
CHASING WISDOM AWAITS.
TRIBAL KNOWLEDGE, VITAL PROBLEMS,
BACK-N-FORTH DEBATES.

ETERNAL RIVALS, SUICIDAL,
COMMITTED DEVOTION TO WHAT'S RELIABLE,
100% UNDENIABLE;
GOD'S VOICE, CALLING FROM THE BIBLE.

II TIMOTHY 3:16-17

16 All Scripture is God-breathed and is useful for teaching, rebuking, correcting and training in righteousness, **17** so that the servant of God may be thoroughly equipped for every good work.

HEBREWS 4:12

12 For the word of God is alive and active. Sharper than any double-edged sword, it penetrates even to dividing soul and spirit, joints and marrow; it judges the thoughts and attitudes of the heart.

ROMANS 8:38-39

38 For I am convinced that neither death nor life, neither angels nor demons, neither the present nor the future, nor any powers, **39** neither height nor depth, nor anything else in all creation, will be able to separate us from the love of God that is in Christ Jesus our Lord.

The Bible is a collection of stories and instructions that will lead you closer to God.

This is "His Word." By reading about God and about His son Jesus, you get a sense of who He is and what He is capable of.

Start a daily reading plan today if you're not already doing so. There's no right or wrong way to go about this—maybe start with just a chapter or two out of one of the Gospels or a daily Proverb. God wants your attention and has so much He wants to share with you. He is ready to use you for good, for the glory of His kingdom...

How can you hear what He has to say if you don't recognize His voice?

He will speak to you through the Bible.

NOT AFRAID

IF THE BREATH IS YOURS,
& THE LUNGS ARE MINE,
THEN I'M FINE, LIVIN' ON BORROWED TIME.
'CAUSE I KNOW I'M NOT ALONE,
& 'NO', I'M NOT AFRAID;
I'M FEELING THE LOVE & THE COMFORT OF THIS PLACE.

WITH OUTSTRETCHED ARMS, THERE'S PEACEFULNESS.
I SENSE YOUR TENDER, WARM HEARTEDNESS.
AS A TODDLER REACHES OUT FOR A HUG,
SO THE HOLY SPIRIT COMES & FILLS ME UP.

IT'S PROMISING, REFRESHING; I'M FEELING THE STRENGTH.
YOU HAVE ME RISING, COURAGEOUSLY, STEPPING OUT IN FAITH,
FOR THE BENEFIT OF OTHERS, THAT THEY MAY SEE YOUR FACE,
THAT THEY MAY KNOW YOUR NAME,
THAT THEY MAY WALK WITHOUT BLAME
& LIVE WITHOUT SHAME.

1 JOHN 3:1

1 See what great love the Father has lavished on us, that we should be called children of God! And that is what we are! The reason the world does not know us is that it did not know him.

1 CORINTHIANS 14:33

33 For God is not a God of disorder but of peace...

JEREMIAH 29:12-14

12 "Then you will call on me and come and pray to me, and I will listen to you. **13** You will seek me and find me when you seek me with all your heart. **14** I will be found by you," declares the LORD, "and I will bring you back from captivity."

JOB 33:4

4 The Spirit of God has made me; the breath of the Almighty gives me life.

Only God knows the plans He has for us. Only He knows why He has brought us out of our reckless lifestyle. Only He knows why we must endure certain struggles in the first place. Giving our hearts and minds over to God relieves us from the need to control, which is in such high demand in our society.

Slow down and back up into the child's role of the family.

Children need lots of attention and care. Children need to be taught everything! How to eat, how to talk, how to behave, what's right, what's wrong. Children need to be disciplined. Children need to fall down and skin their knees. Children need to ask hard questions, and children need to be challenged. Children need a father.

Someone with the "big picture" in mind, the end goal. The one with the answers, the ideas, the strength, the courage to shape and mold us to overcome adversity and rise up out of the fear.

We are the children, and God is the Father in this family; the most loving, gracious Father we've never had here on this earth. He is the most comforting, safe haven we've always desired; the One who can teach, encourage and love us all at the same time. God the Father absolutely LOVES spending time with us. He desires our dependence, and we can come to Him with everything.

I know this will be difficult for some of us, and the purpose isn't to stir up ghosts; it's to remove debilitating influence' that we might correlate with our earthly father and our Heavenly Father. Write a message to God about a time where your earthly father or a father figure has let you down. Ask God to give you healing for this memory and ask Him to come in and fulfill this fatherly role for you. He is waiting to rescue you from the heartache, the resentment, the hurt, and the anguish you have been holding onto.

Far too often we create this idea of who God is based on our earthly relationships and this is a problem because earth is broken and our relationships are flawed. People are selfish and this forces us to become more and more independent so as to not have to deal with everyone's intolerance. God is saying, "No. Rely on me. Come to me as a child, and I will comfort you. Reach out to me when you are scared and trust that I will bend down to where you are and pick you up. I see you child. Here I am."

NOT PERFECT

I'M NOT PERFECT; IN FACT, I'M SICK.
A RECOVERING ADDICT, A DERELICT.
A HOMIE WITH A HARD HEART MADE UP OF BRICKS.

I'M A CONVICT.
CONVICTED DAILY OF MY QUICK-LICKS & ELICIT CONTENT
THAT CONTRADICT THE LIFE JESUS KICKED
READ THE SCRIPT.

MY LIFE IS A BLEND OF BLEMISH' & SCARS.
A COLLAGE OF DARK STAINS & BROKEN PARTS.
TWISTED THOUGHTS, ON 'N OFF THE CHARTS.
BUSTED.
NOW I STAND BEHIND THESE BARS.

I REFLECT & I WRITE.
I CORRECT & I TRY
TO ERECT THRU THE PAIN THIS POSITIVE VIBE.
THIS EMOTIONAL RIDE MAKES ME SPIRITUALLY SMILE,
'CAUSE I KNOW, DEEP INSIDE,
YOU'VE BEEN HERE A WHILE.

THOSE LONG HOURS ON THE BACK ALLEY STREETS
WASN'T EXACTLY WHAT YOU WANTED TO SEE.
IF THERE WAS SOME OTHER WAY, A CHANCE TO BELIEVE,
I KNOW YOU WOULD'VE ALLOWED IT TO BE.

LONG PAST THE STRUGGLES & ON TO RELIEF.
"ALL OF THIS HAPPENED SO THE WORKS OF GOD WOULD BE
DISPLAYED IN [ME]."
REDEEMED!

THANK YOU FOR THE MERCY,
WHICH YOU'VE SO GRACIOUSLY GIVEN
TO THIS UNDESERVING SINNER
& HIS SELF-CENTERED INTENTIONS.
IT'S AS IF YOU HAVE WRITTEN
THESE WORDS FOR YOUR MISSION,
TO CELEBRATE THE GOSPEL & UNITE THE DIVISION.

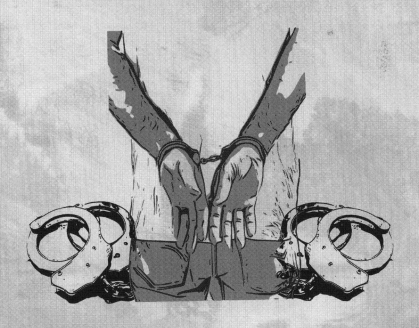

JOHN 9:1-12

(Read the story of Jesus healing a man born blind.)
3"…but this happened so that the works of God might be displayed in him."

EPHESIANS 2:4-5

4 But because of his great love for us, God, who is rich in mercy, 5 made us alive with Christ even when we were dead in transgressions—it is by grace you have been saved.

EPHESIANS 5:4

4 Nor should there be obscenity, foolish talk or coarse joking, which are out of place, but rather thanksgiving.

Congratulations! Not being perfect qualifies you to be used for God's glory. Just think, if God only used perfect people for His Kingdom, He would be lonely and nothing would get done.

Are you ready to accept your flaws as an invitation and start contributing to the benefit of others?

What's the first thing you will do?

Maybe it's some type of service or volunteer work: a community cleanup day, helping out at a local shop, setting up or tearing down at an event, yard work, auto repair… maybe it's as simple as a phone call to check in on a loved one or an old friend…

Your past does not disqualify you from being great! Believers in Christ know they are forgiven of their sins and what God has in store for them is immeasurable. Stop using your past as an excuse for future behavior. Rather, use your past as motivation to propel yourself forward, bringing up those around you simultaneously. If you want change, there has to be change, and you can't blame or expect anyone to do it for you.

FOCUS

IT'S TIME TO FOCUS,
IN ON YOUR VERBS, 'CAUSE THEY KEEP BUZZING AROUND LIKE
BUGGING LOCUSTS.
BREAKING THRU THE DISRUPTIVE STATIC, I CAN'T HELP BUT NOTICE,
THIS PATH, THIS PURPOSE, THIS IDENTITY YOU'RE TRYING TO SHOW US.
HELP ME TO FREE THESE PEOPLE FROM THE DARKNESS LIKE MOSES.

OHHH...
TO BE A FLY ON THE WALL WITNESSING THE TORMENT OF A
HAILSTORM.
THE SLAYING OF THE CATTLE & THE SORROW OF THE FIRSTBORN.
THE BLOODBATH OF DE-'NILE', THE OBVIOUS BEING FOREWARNED.
REFUSING TO LISTEN, SWATTIN' AT THIS GNAT SWARM.

POPPIN' BLISTERS, BOILED FEET,
JUICY MESSAGE EMBEDMENT.
I TRY TO RUN. I TRY TO HIDE,
GOING OUT IN A DIFFERENT DIRECTION.
THE WORD BATTLES, THE COMPROMISE, DELIVERING REJECTION.

OPEN WATERS UNDERFOOT, YELLIN' AT THE CAPTAIN.
CLOAK 'N STAFF, MISSING BOAT, CHOKING ON THE FROG IN THROAT.
MUMBLED WORDS, SPLITTIN' SEAS; I CAN'T BELIEVE WHAT'S
HAPP'NIN'.
LOOKIN' BACK, UNDER ATTACK, THE WAVES COME CRASHIN';
THE ARMIES COLLAPSE.
WE ONCE WAS SLAVES, NOW WE FREE; OH, THE SATISFACTION!

Pharaoh remains, power & fame, his fortunes will consume. When he breathes his last, he's wrapped to last, with the jewelry in his tomb.

I'll call it a lost cause, 'cause you can't take it with, I'll be goin' in an empty box; that's just the way it is.

My treasure's up in Heaven, with my Father & His blessin's, promises, pleasures, inconceivable preparations.

Faith turns the page' of miracles & is why I must commit: my life, to Christ, is an open book, & my name is written in it.

EXODUS CH. 7–14

Read the story of Moses freeing the Israelites from Egypt
[the fastest eight chapters you'll ever read]

MATHEW 6:19–21

19 "Do not store up for yourselves treasures on earth... 20 But store up for yourselves treasures in heaven... 21 For where your treasure is there your heart will be also.

1 TIMOTHY 6:7

7 For we brought nothing into the world, and we can take nothing out of it.

1 CORINTHIANS 2:9

9 ... "What no eye has seen, what no ear has heard, and what no human mind has conceived"

[ISAIAH 64:4]

the things God has prepared for those who love him

REVELATION 20:15

15 Anyone whose name was not found written in the book of life was thrown into the Lake of Fire.

MATTHEW 10:32

32 "Whoever acknowledges me [Jesus] before others, I will also acknowledge before my Father in heaven. But whoever disowns me before others, I will disown before my father in heaven."

First of all, it's important to note, Moses was not perfect. He had a speech impediment.

10 Moses said to the LORD, "Pardon your servant, Lord. I have never been eloquent, neither in the past nor since you have spoken to your servant. I am slow of speech and tongue" (Exodus 4:10).

God's response in verses 11 and 12 is profound. 11 The LORD said to him, "Who gave human beings their mouths? Who makes them deaf or mute? Who gives them sight or makes them blind? Is it not I, the LORD? 12 Now go; I will help you speak and will teach you what to say."

When He calls us to do something, He is going to help us.

You would think this interaction with God would be enough to carry out whatever God is asking, but it's not; not for us and not for Moses. 30 But Moses said to the LORD, "Since I speak with faltering lips, why would Pharaoh listen to me?"' (Exodus 6:30).

God is asking Moses, telling him, rather, to go before Pharaoh, the most powerful man in Egypt, and speak out loud, demanding the freedom of his people or else... "Are you kidding me?! Okay, God, yeah right..." Well, we all know what happens right? There's a series of interactions and plagues described in Exodus, chapters 7–14, and eventually Moses and the Israelites march out of slavery and across the Red Sea to freedom; six hundred thousand men... PLUS women and children (Exodus 12:37)!

So, I have to ask, what "impossible" thing is God asking/telling you to do?

What insecurity/fear is temporarily holding you back?

When you put your own comfort and understanding off to the side and put God first, trusting in His word, believing in His capabilities, this faith is what will lead you out of captivity and into freedom— miraculous achievement beyond comprehension.

When you trust God and love others, when you stop taking yourself so seriously and realize it's not all about 'me', you are putting Jesus first. When you put Jesus first, you rely on Him, and when you rely on Him, He gives you His power. When you use His power for His will here on earth, just imagine what He will share with you in Heaven! Then realize, Heaven will be far greater than everything you just imagined!

CONSTANTLY ABRASIVE

CONSTANTLY ABRASIVE; LET'S FACE IT.
THIS PAINSTAKING, FORCIBLY UNHAPPY WAY OF LIFE—LET'S STOP FAKING!
SYSTEMIC BRAIN WAVE HACKING.
MIND CONTROL RACKING.
YOUR THOUGHTS CREATE ACTIONS & IT'S A MENTAL HIJACKING.
I'M CRACKING!
UP & OUT OF THIS PLACE,
IT'S NOT SAFE.
IT'S GOT ME IN THIS VULNERABLE STATE.
MY EMOTIONS ARE ABOUT READY TO BREAK.
SO MY WORDS SPRAY OUT & DENT THIS PAGE,
OF PAPER IN MY BOOK,
THERE'S ONLY ONE PLACE TO LOOK,
& IT'S UP...
UP TO YOU, LORD.
FOR YOUR HELP & YOUR HAND,
YOU ENCOURAGE ME TO STAND,
AGAINST THE EVIL IN THIS LAND.
YOU'RE TELLING ME YOUR PLAN,
THE THAT & THE THIS;
YOU HAVE ME BALLIN' UP MY FISTS,
SO I CAN FIGHT BACK AGAINST THIS CULTURAL TWIST.
THIS TORNADO OF DECEPTION, I CAN'T QUITE GRIP,
& IT SLIPS & IT RIPS & IT THROWS ME AROUND,
'TIL I'M FIGHTIN' FOR MY LIFE, LYING HERE ON THE GROUND.
I'M BEGGIN' FOR YOUR PEACE, ASKIN' PRETTY PRETTY PLEASE,
& IT'S CALM...
THE WIND SLOWS TO A BREEZE.

THE TWIGS STAY ON THE TREES.
& ALL THE PAIN LEAVES...
YOUR SPIRIT COMES DOWN TO ME
& FILLS ME UP.
YOUR WORDS HOLD ME TIGHTLY... I'M STUCK,
IN YOUR ARMS, & YOU'RE ASKIN' ALL THE WHILE,
"WHY DO YOU TRY TO FIGHT THIS ON YOUR OWN EVERY TIME?"
"...'CAUSE I'M A CHILD... LORD... I'M YOUR CHILD."

GALATIANS 4:6-7

6 ...God sent the Spirit of his Son into our hearts... 7 So you are no longer a slave, but God's child; and since you are his child, God has also made you an heir [to the kingdom].

JOHN 1:12

12 Yet to all who did receive him, to those who believed in his name, he gave the right to become children of God.

MATTHEW 8:23-27

[Jesus Calms the Storm]

23 Then he got into the boat and his disciples followed him. 24 Suddenly a furious storm came up on the lake, so that the waves swept over the boat. But Jesus was sleeping. 25 The disciples went and woke him saying, "Lord, save us! We're going to drown!" 26 He replied, "You of little faith, why are you so afraid?" Then he got up and rebuked the winds and the waves, and it was completely calm. 27 The men were amazed and asked, "What kind of man is this? Even the winds and the waves obey him!"

MARK 14:38

[Jesus said] 38 "Watch and pray so that you will not fall into temptation. The Spirit is willing, but the flesh is weak."

What storms are you trying to fight by yourself? Is there a storm at work? At home? In a relationship? Some form of addiction? How much longer are you going to fight it alone? Jesus is waiting for you to wake Him up so he can "calm your storm." He wants to help you; just call out His name.

"Jesus, I don't know really know how this works. I just know I'm tired, and I can't do this on my own anymore. I've done everything I can, and it's not working. Please come into my life right now and save me from this storm."

STRADDLED BOTH SIDES

I'VE STRADDLED BOTH SIDES
& STRUGGLED WITH THE IN-BETWEENS.
I'VE BATTLED BOLD LIES,
MUDDLED WITH HALLUCINOGENIC DREAMS.

I'VE ENCOUNTERED SLEEPLESS NIGHTS THAT TURNED INTO WEEKS
& FLOUNDERED HUMAN RIGHTS WITH MY OWN DISBELIEF.

STRONG-WILLED & A ONE-TRACK MIND,
I PUT ME FIRST, EVERY SINGLE TIME.

A BOWL OF DIRTY WATER BEING FLUSHED DOWN THE DRAIN,
A WAY OUT, SURF'S UP; YEAH, I RODE THAT WAVE.
WAS TOO EASY, A WAY TO ESCAPE WITH NO PAIN.

WHOOPS, HOLE-SHOT, NO LOOKIN' BACK,
SELF-DESTRUCTION ON THIS RACE TRACK.
'BRAAT BRAAAAT', FULL SPEED AHEAD,
THROWING DIRT CLODS & ROCKS,
BLOWING SMOKE, FULL SEND.

BUT THERE WAS SOMETHIN' STIRRIN' IN MY MIND
ABOUT WAXIN' THAT KIND OF GRIND,
I WAS SKATIN' THRU LIFE, YET I WAS FALLIN' BEHIND.
MY DREAMS WERE OUT OF REACH;
I WAS EMPTY INSIDE.

I NEEDED NEW EYES, SOME SPARK OF LIGHT,
A REMINDER THAT I'M NOT ALONE IN THIS FIGHT.
A GLIMPSE OF HOPE THAT IT'S GONNA BE ALL RIGHT.
BECAUSE YA SEE, I ONCE BELIEVED
THAT I'M PERFECT IN HIS SIGHT.

YEAH, NOW IT'S COMIN' BACK; THAT'S A FACT.
THERE IS A GOD, A ONE TRUE KING.
HE LEFT THE 99 & CAME LOOKIN' FOR ME!

SEE, I ONCE WAS LOST; NOW I'M JUST JOSH,
& I THANK THE LORD,
HE'S THE COUNSELOR OF MY CHAOS.

LUKE 15:1-7

1 Now the tax collectors and sinners were all gathering around to hear Jesus. **2** But the Pharisees and the teachers of the law muttered, "This man welcomes sinners and eats with them." **3** Then Jesus told them this parable: **4** "Suppose one of you has a hundred sheep and loses one of them. Doesn't he leave the ninety-nine in the open country and go after the lost sheep until he finds it? **5** And when he finds it he joyfully puts it on his shoulders **6** and goes home. Then he calls his friends and neighbors together and says, 'Rejoice with me; I have found my lost sheep.' **7** I tell you that in the same way there will be more rejoicing in heaven over one sinner who repents than over ninety-nine righteous persons who do not need to repent."

JEREMIAH 31:34

34 ... "For I will forgive their wickedness and will remember their sins no more."

COLOSSIANS 1:22

22 But now he has reconciled you by Christ's physical body through death to present you holy in his sight, without blemish and free from accusation...

MATTHEW 9:12-13

12 ...Jesus said, "It is not the healthy who need a doctor, but the sick. **13** But go and learn what this means: 'I desire mercy, not sacrifice.' For I have not come to call the righteous, but sinners."

LUKE 19:10

10 For the Son of Man came to seek and to save the lost.

No matter what your past looks like, Jesus loves you. Whatever sin is holding you down, wherever you might be feeling trapped, Jesus knows about it and wants to free you from that pain and confusion. He bought your life at a price. Do you know what that means? It means your life is of value to Him. You are adequate in His eyes. You matter to Him, and He wants you to know this.

If you're suffering from some type of addiction or betrayal, some form of sexual immorality or confused identity, you are exactly the type of person Jesus came to save. At any moment you can turn from your "wicked" ways and start following Jesus. He will not only forgive you of your sins. He tells us He "will remember [them] no more—" Like they never even happened... Praise God!

DECIDUOUS BY NATURE

DECIDUOUS BY NATURE.
GROWING OUT OF MY INSIDIOUS BEHAVIOR.
INVESTING IN MY FAMILY, DEVOTED TO MY CREATOR.
LEARNIN' TO BE A PRUDENT, INTROVERTED SPECTATOR.
SEEIN' THINGS HOW THEY ARE & DOIN' THINGS HOW THEY OUGHT
TO BE DONE...
WHAT A GAME CHANGER.

I HAVE TO PAUSE. I HAVE TO BE STILL.
I'M NOT LIVIN' FOR ME ANYMORE;
THIS IS GOD'S WILL.

THIS BUSTED-UP BODY IS BREAKING DOWN FAST.
I'M 'BOUT A SLIVER AWAY FROM BEING HANDICAPPED.
HERE, LISTEN TO THIS; I DON'T CARE IF YOU LAUGH.
I PUT SOME OUTDOOR FURNITURE TOGETHER,
FELT LIKE I NEEDED AN ICE BATH.
NOW I'M WAKIN' UP WITH THESE SLEEPY, TINGLY HANDS,
DOCTOR SAYS CARPAL TUNNEL; I'M ONLY THIRTY-FOUR, MAN.
I GUESS SOME THINGS ARE NOT MEANT FOR US TO UNDERSTAND.

THIS DOESN'T MAKE ME MAD AT GOD, FOR HEAVEN'S SAKE;
IT'S JUST A CONSTANT REMINDER THAT I NEED MORE OF HIS
STRENGTH.
"ASK & YOU SHALL RECEIVE,"
& HE'S CHECKIN' OFF THE BOXES FASTER THAN I CAN SAY "PLEASE."

AND THIS IS WHY I FOLLOW JESUS; YA HEARD?
HE CAME INTO THIS WORLD TO SERVE, NOT TO BE SERVED.
NOT AS A ROYAL, GLAMOROUS KING,

BUT AS A LOYAL, REBELLIOUS, MAN OF THE STREET.
HE WASHED PEOPLE'S FEET & FED THE HUNGRY WITH HARDLY
NOTHIN' TO EAT.
HE STOOD UP AGAINST THE RELIGIOUS GOVERNMENT,
THE PHARISEES,
& MORE IMPORTANTLY,
JESUS LIVED OUT HIS FATHER'S DREAM
& PREDICTED HIS OWN DEATH, DOWN TO THE 't,'
WHICH HAPPENS TO BE A CROSS, WHERE HE WAS CRUCIFIED,
NAILED UP ON THAT TREE.
HE GAVE UP HIS OWN LIFE FOR YOU & ME,
SO WE, COULD BE, IN HEAVEN WITH HIM, FOR ETERNITY!
THIS ISN'T JUST BIBLE STORIES; IT'S OUR HISTORY.
THE WHOLE RECORD OF TIME IS BASED ON HIS EXISTENCE.
BC-AD—THE WESTERN WORLD FOR INSTANCE.

SO DON'T BE HOSTILE TO THE GOSPEL & DON'T GET IT TWISTED,
I DON'T HAVE TO DEFEND JESUS; I'M HERE TO DELIVER HIS MESSAGE.

IT'S SPELLED OUT PRETTY CLEAR & ACTUALLY QUITE PASSIONATE,
SACRIFICIAL LOVE & ACTIVELY COMPASSIONATE.

A NEVER-ENDING SEARCH PARTY FOR SINNERS & THE LIKE.
A CELEBRATION IN HEAVEN WHEN THE BROKEN FIND NEW LIFE.
DIDACTIC INTERVENTION, THE HOLY SPIRIT INTERTWINED...

NO MOUNTAIN IS TOO STEEP.
NO VALLEY IS TOO DEEP.
BECAUSE, GOD'S LIMITS, ARE FROM OUR OWN DISBELIEF...
SO I BELIEVE.

PSALM 46:10

10 He says, "Be still, and know that I am God…"

MARK 11:24

24 "…Therefore I tell you, whatever you ask for in prayer, believe that you have received it, and it will be yours."

MATTHEW 20:18–19

18 "…the Son of Man will be delivered over to the chief priests and the teachers of the law. They will condemn him to death **19** and will hand him over to the Gentiles to be mocked and flogged and crucified. On the third day he will be raised to life!"

II PETER 3:9

9 The Lord is not slow in keeping his promise, as some understand slowness. Instead he is patient with you, not wanting anyone to perish, but everyone to come to repentance.

We all want "more." We all want "better." We all push, sell, persuade, and manipulate others to be more in line with our own way of thinking, with our philosophy, with our ideology. When we want things that are not in line with what God wants, we start wandering off-track. Eventually, more often than not, we hit a wall or worse… rock bottom.

Maybe some of us are at bottom right now. Let me tell you from experience what that felt like for me: miserable, painful, helpless, hopeless. I felt trapped, stuck, wrapped in negativity. I felt scared, ashamed, angry, confused. I felt alone, embarrassed, anxious, depressed, unwanted. I felt dirty, suicidal. I was surrounded by darkness… empty.

This is what it feels like to be separated from God.

When Jesus hung on that cross and died for our sins, this is exactly what he felt for ALL of humanity. He took on all of this pain and suffering; He paid the ultimate price for our sins so we wouldn't have to. We are flawed at birth. We are born into a broken world. God knew that we would NEVER be able to make it into Heaven on our own, so He put together a rescue mission to save us from ourselves.

You might ask yourself, "Why would God want to save me?" Because He loves you! You are special to Him. He created you and wants to spend time with you. Do you not love the things you create? Artwork? Music? Clothing styles? Hairstyles? Car modifications? Home improvement projects? Your own children?

When you spend time with God, He reveals Himself to you.

As you begin to understand who God is, He allows you to experience the glory of His goodness. Believe it or not, you were created with intention. He has designed you with specific skills. When you use those talents and those skills for what God intended them to be used for, you bring pleasure to God. When you bring pleasure to God, He will bless you... That's a promise!

What are some of your skills? What are some things you are good at? Thank God for what you have and ask Him how He wants you to be using those gifts. When you start consulting with God and walking with Him, you actually start walking away from all of those negative emotions that have been haunting you. Don't take my word for it; I can't change your mind. Only the Holy Spirit can do that.

IF I COULD PAY ATTENTION

THE PAIN WOULD GO AWAY, IF I COULD ONLY LISTEN.
ALL OF THIS WOULD CHANGE, IF I COULD PAY ATTENTION.

YOU'VE GIVEN ME, IDENTITY,
A ROAD MAP TO, ETERNITY.
I TRAVEL UNDER YOUR PROVISION.
I TRUST YOU ON THIS MISSION.
HELP ME JUST TO LISTEN.

LET YOUR WORDS REST IN MY EAR;
LET YOUR PEACE REST IN MY HEART;
LET YOUR PROMISE' REST THIS FEAR,
BEFORE I FALL APART.

I KNOW LIFE ISN'T PAINLESS;
I'D RATHER FEEL YOUR LOVE INSTEAD.
HELP ME TO LET GO OF TOMORROW,
& REMOVE THE DARKNESS FROM MY HEAD.

LET YOUR WORDS REST IN MY EAR;
LET YOUR PEACE REST IN MY HEART,
LET YOUR PROMISE' REST THIS FEAR,
BEFORE I FALL APART.

JOHN 16:33

33 "I [Jesus] have told you these things, so that in me you may have peace. In this world you will have trouble. But take heart! I have overcome the world."

COLOSSIANS 3:2

2 Set your minds on things above, not on earthly things.

MATTHEW 6:34

34 "Therefore do not worry about tomorrow, for tomorrow will worry about itself…"

JEREMIAH 29:11

11 "For I know the plans I have for you," declares the Lord, "plans to prosper you and not to harm you, plans to give you hope and a future.

MATTHEW 19:26

26 Jesus looked at them and said, "With man this is impossible, but with God all things are possible."

This is a call to action. We have an important role to play here for ourselves, for our families, for our friends, for the Kingdom of Heaven. To understand this important role, we must first listen and pay attention.

God doesn't demand that we do anything; that would be abuse. When we look to Him, He delivers encouragement. Sometimes this motivation will make sense; it will be easy to understand AND follow through with. Other times, the ideas can be more difficult to understand, and we are reluctant to follow through because of what others might think, or we believe we can't, or it's impossible… Well, nothing is impossible with God, and He always wants what's best for us.

What has been pressing on your heart lately? What call to action have you been going back 'n forth on? What area of life feels like a big circle? Round 'n round, same ol', same ol'. There's no progress, no growth, stagnant…

Listen! Pay attention! Follow through. Ask for help from your Heavenly Father. Ask for wisdom. Ask for understanding.

APPLES & ORANGES

APPLES & ORANGES.
THIS JESUS ADORES YA.
HE HUNG ON THAT CROSS & MOURNED YA.
THE TRUTH IS IN THE WORD & IT WARNS YA.
THE WAS & IS & IS TO COME,
ETERNAL LIFE WITH THE FATHER & THE SON.
THE PLACE IS PREPARED;
HE'S EXPECTING YOU THERE.
PARADISE & GLORY WILL DEFINITELY BE SHARED.
HE'S PLANNING YOUR REVIVAL,
AWAITING YOUR ARRIVAL,
THE FAITH YOU MAY HAVE, IS GOING TO BE VITAL.

BACK TO THE APPLES; IT'S TIME TO MAKE SOME SAUCE.
SATAN WILL FIND YOU; HE'LL STOP AT NO COST.
HE'LL FILL YOU WITH LIES, DIVIDE YOUR THOUGHTS,
DISTRACT YOUR EMOTIONS, 'TIL YOU'RE TOTALLY LOST.
HE REIGNS WITH DECEIT, A FALSE HOPE YOU BELIEVE.
WHEN YOU STUMBLE AND FALL, HE'S NOWHERE TO BE SEEN.

SO DON'T BELIEVE THE HYPE, THE IMAGE, OR THE TYPE.
THE PERSON YOU BECOME, DOESN'T HAPPEN OVERNIGHT.
IT'S NOT IN YOUR CLOTHES; IT'S NOT IN YOUR RIDE,
THE JOB THAT YOU CHOSE, OR THE SECRETS THAT YOU HIDE.
THESE ARE SATAN'S TOOLS; SHOULDN'T COME AS A SURPRISE.
DOLLAR SIGNS AND PRICE TAGS WILL ALWAYS COLLIDE,
WITH THE PROPER WAY OF THINKING; WE ALL MUST DECIDE.

SO, IF YOU CHOOSE COMFORT, I HOPE YOU STAY COMFORTABLE.
& IF YOU CHOOSE CHARACTER, YOU'RE GONNA BE VULNERABLE.

DON'T GIVE UP YET; LET'S SET THE STORY STRAIGHT.
YOUR MIND IS A BATTLEFIELD, FOR WHAT YOU CONTEMPLATE.
WHEN YOU ACCEPT CHRIST'S LOVE, THE SPIRIT COMES AWAKE.
IT FINDS YOU & GUIDES YOU, THRU THE CHOICES THAT YOU MAKE.

IT LEADS YOU & FREES YOU, FROM YOUR NATURAL SINFUL WAYS,
ENCOURAGING SUGGESTIONS, DIRECTLY TO YOUR BRAIN.

SO COME CLEAN, COME OUT, REMOVE YOUR SELF-DOUBT.
LET GO, LET GOD, IS WHAT IT'S ALL ABOUT.

IT'S YOUR CHOICE; IT'S FREE WILL.
YOU'RE NOT FORCED TO LOVE HIM,
BUT HE LOVES YOU STILL.

EITHER WAY, HE'S GOT PLANS.
READY TO MEET YOU WITH OPEN HANDS.
KNOW BEFORE YOU GO;
DON'T LEAVE IT UP TO CHANCE.

REVELATION 1:8

8 "I am the Alpha and the Omega," says the Lord God, "who is, and who was, and who is to come, the Almighty."

JOHN 14:2-3

2 "My Father's house has many rooms;... I am going there to prepare a place for you 3 ... if I go and prepare a place for you, I will come back and take you to be with me that you also may be where I am."

REVELATION 12:9

9 The great dragon was hurled down—that ancient serpent called the Devil, or Satan, who leads the whole world astray. He was hurled to the Earth and his angels with him.

HEBREWS 13:5

5 Keep your lives free from the love of money and be content with what you have, because God has said, "Never will I leave you; Never will I forsake you."
DEUT. 31:6

ROMANS 8:26-27

26 In the same way, the Spirit helps us in our weakness. We do not know what we ought to pray for, but the Spirit himself intercedes for us through wordless groans. 27 And he who searches our hearts knows the mind of the Spirit, because the Spirit intercedes for God's people in accordance with the will of God.

Life is terminal. No one will make it out alive. Are you living a life that will guarantee you a room in Heaven? A room Jesus says He is preparing for you? Or, are you approaching the day-to-day based on your own feelings, your own standards, your own comforts and your own ideas? Wouldn't you agree that this temporary life isn't all that it's cracked up to be? Jesus wants to spend eternity with you, and He's giving you access to His spirit, the Holy Spirit, to help you until that day. Whenever you're ready to tap into that power, all you have to do is ask.

Stop pretending that this is all you have. Stop trying to 'live your best life' now. The best is yet to come and it will not be achieved by the work of your hands.

Spend some time thanking Jesus for what He has done and ask the Holy Spirit to silence the noise in your head so you can hear the next move.

DON'T BE AFRAID

SOCIAL DISTORTION' BEEN MY NORMAL FOR 20 YEARS.
ALL THIS LOCAL, EMOTIONAL OUTRAGE HAS ME FEELIN' PRETTY
CERTAIN END TIMES ARE NEAR.
THE NATURAL DISASTERS, THE FAMINES, THE PLAGUES;
THESE "BIRTHING PAINS" ARE MAKIN' IT QUITE CLEAR.

THIS SOBER JUNKIE IS NO LONGER CHOKIN' ON SUBSTANCE OR
SLAMMIN' DOWN BEERS TO DROWN OUT THE F.E.A.R.
—False Evidence Appearing Real—
DID I JUST DROP THAT ACROSTIC HERE?
I BEEN PUTTIN' MY HOPE IN A HIGH PLACE & WATCHIN' ALL MY
DESPERATION DISAPPEAR.

I WRAP MY BIBLE IN A BROWN PAPER BAG & CHUG IT LIKE A 40 [OZ].
I EVEN POUR A LIL' OUT FOR THE HOMIES & SPILL SOME TRUTH
INTO THEIR STORY.

PEOPLE HAVE BECOME "LOVERS OF THEMSELVES,"
HOLDIN' EACH OTHER IN CONTEMPT & PROPAGATIN' HATE.
INVOLVED IN A NEVER—ENDING DEBACLE OF DEBATE; BUT WAIT,
BEST NOT CONGREGATE, LEST YOUR EGO BE TRIED WITH IMPLICIT
RESTRAINT.
THERE'S NO ESCAPE.

// HELP ME TO BOUNCE BACK FROM INSULTS, NEGATIVITY HURLED.
ALLOW ME TO FORGET, FORGET THIS BROKEN WORLD. //

THE MEDICAL PROPAGANDA IS INSANE.
THE IDEOLOGY IS DERANGED.
IT'S WORLDLY & SCIENTIFICALLY PROVEN TO CHANGE...
ONLY JESUS CAN SAVE.

I'M SICK OF THE CONTRADICTIONS, THE HYPOCRITICAL DIVISIONS,
THE PRIVATE SECTOR ENTERPRISE' DEFENDING THESE ALGORITHMS.

I'M FLABBERGASTED; DONE WITH THESE SLAVERY TACTICS;
PULLIN' MUSCLES DOIN' MENTAL GYMNASTICS.
THESE POLITICAL ANTICS WON'T GRANT'CHA HEAVENLY PASSAGE...
THEY PLAYIN' SAVAGE!

THE WORLD IS POLLUTED, CONVOLUTED, & TOXIC.
TRUST & TRUTH IS DILUTED & OBNOXIOUS.
WILL WE EVER GET BACK TO COMMON SENSE OR LOGIC?
NOT WHEN WE LIVE AMONG SENSELESS COMMONS... IT'S NOSTALGIC.

"YOUR BODY, MY CHOICE" IS THE NEW MESSAGE BEING SPOKE
WITH THE PROGRAMMED VOICE.
NOW I'M RESPONSIBLE FOR YOUR IMMUNE SYSTEM?
...REMINDS ME OF THE BETRAYAL OF JESUS WHEN JUDAS
[LAVISHLY] KISSED HIM.

I'M NOT SAYIN' WE JUST THROW COMMON COURTESY OUT THE WINDOW.
I AM TRYIN' TO PROMOTE WE FREE OUR MINDS FROM
THREATENING INNUENDOS...
THERE'S MILLIONS OF PEOPLE OUT THERE ALLERGIC TO PEANUTS,
& THEY STILL MASS PRODUCIN' PEANUT BUTTER, ADVERTISIN'
WE EAT IT.

WE'RE LIVIN' APPREHENSIVELY BEHIND A ONE-WORLD VIEW.
BEIN' FORCED TO FILL THESE IMMORAL SHOES.
SIDE-STEPPIN' PROBLEMS & APPLYING BAND-AIDS TO AREAS NOT
INTENDED FOR USE.
IT'S ABUSE!

UNDER A STATE OF CONSTANT RIDICULE. IT'S CRUEL,
& UNUSUAL PUNISHMENT.
SO, I INVITE YOU, WITH A MESSAGE OF SENTIMENT,
TO STOP RECYCLING THE NEWS OF YOUR ENVIRONMENT.

SEEK OUT A REASON FOR THE SUFFERING & A DREAM THAT GOES
ALONG WITH THE PAIN.
CEASE THE MENTAL SHUFFLING & TEAM WITH THE SUPREME
BEING, BRINGING POSITIVITY OUT OF HUMBLE CHANGE.

// EXTRAPOLATE THE NONSENSE; DESTROY THE DIS-BELIEF.
ISOLATE THE VIOLENCE; SILENCE THE INVASIVE SPEECH. //

ARE WE REALLY GONNA KEEP LIVING OUR DAYS SPREADING
DIVISIVE COMPLAINTS,
OR DO WE HAVE A DIFFERENCE TO MAKE, WITH AN EYE ON THE
END GAME?
WE'RE A LIMITED SPECIES WITH AN EXPIRATION DATE,
& OUR INTERNAL CLOCK IS TICK-TOCKING AWAY.

I'M SAYIN' THIS WITH AN OPEN MIND. I PRAY YOU'LL RECEIVE IT
WITH ONE TOO:
THIS IS HOPE, THIS' SINCERE, A REMINDER, JESUS LOVES YOU.

DON'T BE AFRAID.

PSALM 56:3-4

3 When I am afraid, I put my trust in you **4** ...What can mere mortals do to me?

JAMES 1:27

27 ...Keep [yourself] from being polluted by the world.

LUKE 21:11

11 There will be great earthquakes, famines, and pestilences in various places, and fearful events and great signs from heaven.

MARK 13:7-8

7 When you hear of wars and rumors of wars, do not be alarmed. Such things must happen, but the end is still to come. **8** Nation will rise against nation, and kingdom against kingdom. There will be earthquakes in various places, and famines. These are the beginning of birth pains.

2 TIMOTHY 3:1-5

1 ...There will be terrible times in the last days. **2** People will be lovers of themselves, lovers of money, boastful, proud, abusive, disobedient to their parents, ungrateful, unholy, **3** without love, unforgiving, slanderous, without self-control, brutal, not lovers of the good, **4** treacherous, rash, conceited, lovers of pleasure rather than lovers of God - **5** having a form of godliness but denying its power. Have nothing to do with such people.

MATTHEW 26:48-50

48 Now the betrayer had arranged a signal with them: "The one I kiss is the man; arrest him." **49** Going at once to Jesus, Judas said, "Greetings, Rabbi!" and kissed him. **50** Jesus replied, "Do what you came for friend."

MARK 5:36

36 ...Jesus told him, "Don't be afraid; just believe."

All throughout the Bible, God tells us believers, "Do not be afraid." We don't have to be afraid because we have faith in God, in His security, because God is faithful to His children. What does this mean exactly? It means no matter what happens, we are never alone. Someone always has our back. Someone is always ready to 'throw down' for us. Someone is always praying for us. Someone is always there to listen to us, and someone is always there to love us un-conditionally—even when we screw-up, backslide, or relapse. That someone is Jesus.

When Jesus is number one in our life, there is nothing to be afraid of; for even if we die, He will give us life. (John 11:25) Amen? Amen.

If you are not a believer, then, yes, I would be afraid. "If you are not for God, then you are against Him" (Matthew 12:30). Seeing as how God is a God of justice, He will see to it that evil is punished, and the upright will be rewarded accordingly. We all want justice, right? Justice in the streets. Justice in the courts. Justice for specific groups. What about justice for yourself? What will that really look like?

At the time of writing—September 2021—it's not hard to notice, the world is an absolute mess. Rules, regulations, and health frustrations are constantly changing. We need to be overly mindful of everyone else's needs rather than being responsible for ourselves. Our freedoms are being stripped, and our free will is being taken away. Our privacy is almost non-existent, mostly by choice as we self-promote on social media, subjecting ourselves to the algorithmic sharing of our personal information and advertising. We're practically leading ourselves into slavery by being so plugged in to our favorite podcasts, news and TV channels, music, books, etc., listening to these narratives telling us how to live… (this book being no exception). You gotta ask yourself, "Who or what is the influence? What is the promotion? Who does this benefit?" Ultimately, "Why am I giving my time to this idea?"

Ironically, we are living in this predicament because God won't take away our free will. We are free to love Him, follow Him, and serve Him. We are also free to indulge in the flesh, provoke hate, and be proud of our material possessions…

It's not up to us to fix any type of worldly problem. It is up to us, however, to decide if we want to secure eternal salvation. You can make that decision right now if you haven't already; just pray this prayer:

Dear God, Father in Heaven, thank you for giving me free will. I have been living a life according to my own desires, my own expectations, and something is missing. Will you please come into my heart right now? I'm desperate for something more. I'm ready to experience what You have to offer. I still have a lot of questions, and I'm ready for You to start answering them. I'm not perfect, and I believe You can help with this part too. Will you please forgive me of my sins? The ones I know about and the ones I'm not even aware of. Please help me to see things from Your perspective so that I don't have to live in fear. In Your Son Jesus's name. Amen.

GRAFF STANCE

MATHEMATICAL, SCIENTIFIC, & SUPERNATURAL.
LIKE CANS OF PAINT,
HEARTS ARE GONNA SHAKE,
HEADS ARE GONNA RATTLE.
BEST TO CLAIM YO' SET FOR THIS SPIRITUAL BATTLE.

I'M SPRAYIN' TRUTH FROM THE START,
TAGGIN' SCRIPTURES ON MY HEART
& THROWIN' UP ETERNAL VERSES THAT'LL NEVER BE TORN APART.

I'MMA GET A CAN O' IRONLAK & A FAT CAP
& COVER UP THE OUTLINE OF MY PAST
WITH THIS COMPRESSED GAS…
'CAUSE I DON'T NEED THAT.

I'VE BEEN RENEWED.
JUST LETTIN' MY MEMORIES BE RE-USED
SO THAT OTHERS MIGHT PUT THEMSELVES UNDER RE-VIEW
& TAKE THE NEXT STEPS AT GETTING TO KNOW YOU.

THE SLATE'S BEEN WIPED CLEAN;
I FOCUS ON WHAT IS UNSEEN
& PIECE UP MY BELIEFS LIKE SOME TYPE OF JESUS FREAK.

I PRAY YOU'LL LET THESE WORDS LEAK
STRAIGHT TO YOUR FRONTAL CORTEX
& LET THE HOLY SPIRIT SPEAK,
SOME TYPE OF FAITHFUL VORTEX
'TIL YOU TURN & SEE,
JESUS CHILLIN' ON YOUR DOORSTEP.

HAD TO JUMP OFF THE FENCE & DECIDE.
I COULDN'T HIDE.
THE LIGHT WAS SO BRIGHT; IT BLINDED MY EYES.
WAS TIRED OF TRYIN' TO SLIDE INTO SOCIETY'S DESIGN,
SO I'M BUFFIN' OUT THE WORLD'S DISGUISE.
I'M NOT BUYIN' THE LIES;
THE HUMAN BODY IS BORN TO DIE.
TIME TO BUST OUT THE STEEL SCRIBE
& ETCH INTO MY RIGHT SIDE:
SOCIAL NORMS INFECT LIFE!

2 CORINTHIANS 4:16-18

16 Therefore we do not lose heart. Though outwardly we are wasting away, yet inwardly we are being renewed day by day. **17** For our light and momentary troubles are achieving for us an eternal glory that far outweighs them all. **18** So we fix our eyes not on what is seen but what is unseen, since what is seen is temporary, but what is unseen is eternal.

ROMANS 10:9-10

9 If you declare with your mouth, "Jesus is Lord," and believe in your heart that God raised him from the dead, you will be saved. **10** For it is with your heart that you believe and are justified, and it is with your mouth that you profess your faith and are saved.

EPHESIANS 1:13-14

13 ...When you believed, you were marked in him with a seal, the promised Holy Spirit, **14** who is a deposit guaranteeing our inheritance until the redemption of those who are God's possession—to the praise of His glory.

What is driving your lifestyle? Are you being influenced by what is socially acceptable or "normal"? Are you letting today's culture tell you what is missing from your life? Or why you need a certain product to feel better about yourself? To feel accepted? Jesus offers truth and life. Jesus wants to meet you wherever you are in your life; you don't have to get cleaned up first. You just need to acknowledge certain areas in your life need attention and ask Jesus to come into those areas to help. Allow the Holy Spirit to guide you through this process.

For real, though, what's bothering you? What's lingering in your mind? Some form of worry or anticipation? Write this feeling down and talk to God about it. The creator of the universe wants to talk life with you and walk through your questions with you. Dedicate some time for these appointments. Jesus' schedule is wide open...

RINSE & REPEAT

CONSTRUCTED. CONFLICTED.
CORRUPTED. ENCRYPTED.
ABDUCTED. ADDICTED.
REJECTED. CONVICTED.
FORBIDDEN. BED-RIDDEN.
SUBMITTED. UN-FRIENDED.

CONTENDED. SURRENDERED.
REPENTED. REMEMBERED.

PLEASE REMEMBER ME, JESUS, MY KING.
MY HOPEFUL REDEEMER, MY REFUGE, CONCRETE.

MY CONFIDENCE, COMMON SENSE.
DELIVERANCE, FROM THE SUSPENSE.

THIS DAILY ROUTINE.
THIS RENOVATION OF ME.
MY BODY, YOUR TEMPLE.
RINSE & REPEAT.

MATTHEW 6:9-13

9 ... "Our Father in heaven, hallowed be your name, **10** your kingdom come, your will be done, on earth as it is in heaven. **11** Give us today our daily bread. **12** And forgive us our debts, as we also have forgiven our debtors. **13** And lead us not into temptation, but deliver us from the evil one."

1 CORINTHIANS 6:19-20

19 Do you not know that your bodies are temples of the Holy Spirit, who is in you, whom you have received from God? You are not your own; **20** you were bought at a price. Therefore honor God with your bodies.

ISAIAH 49:15-16

15 "... I will not forget you! **16** See, I have engraved you on the palms of my hands..."

Today is a new day, and tomorrow never comes. Ask God, "Who am I today?"

Let Him prepare your thoughts. Ask Him to reveal Himself to you. Let God tell you what's on the agenda. Ask questions. Listen. This is a relationship, not a regimen. You can talk to God just as you would talk to a family member or a friend. Tell Him what makes you happy. Tell Him what makes you mad. Tell Him when something is funny. Prayer doesn't always have be pleading for a miracle; in fact, chances are, if we're begging for a miracle, something is probably terribly wrong, and God never wants to see His children hurting.

We're not designed to understand or worry about the future, and we're certainly not capable of carrying the burdens of our past. Let that go and live for today.

When we maintain an open line of communication with our Father in Heaven, we get to enjoy how He is interacting in our daily routine. When we adjust our focus to Him, we will be able to witness just how focused He is on us. Try it out.

BREAK AWAY

TRYING TO BREAK AWAY,
BREAK FREE FROM MY OLD WAYS.
TRYING TO CHANGE MY DAYS,
TRANSFORM MY OLD BRAIN.
STRUGGLING TO BREAK AWAY;
PLEASE GIVE ME YOUR STRENGTH TODAY.
MY WILL IS FADING AWAY;
I NEED YOUR SPIRIT TO STAY.

I KNOW YOU FEEL MY PAIN.
YOU TOLD ME, "JESUS WEPT."
HE DIED FOR MY SINS;
I WASN'T EVEN BORN YET.

LOST BUT NOT FORGOTTEN.
ALONE BUT NOT ABANDONED.
TRAPPED IN THIS UNCLEAN WORLD,
LIVING OUT WHAT YOU'VE COMMANDED.

I GET 1 THRU 10; THESE CAME FROM ABOVE,
& THEN JESUS SAID, 'THE GREATEST ONE IS LOVE.'

SO HERE I STAND IN AWE,
AT THE LOVE YOU HAVE FOR ME,
A JAW-DROPPING PAUSE,
FOR THE HOPE OF ETERNITY.

CREATED IN YOUR IMAGE,
HEEDING YOUR DIRECTION,
I GAZE INTO THE HEAVENS,
SEEING YOUR REFLECTION.

JOHN 11:35

35 Jesus wept.

ROMANS 5:6, 8

6 ...when we were still powerless, Christ died for the un-Godly... **8** God demonstrates his own love for us in this: While we were still sinners, Christ died for us.

MARK 12:29-31

29 "The most important one," answered Jesus, "is this: '... **30** Love the Lord your God with all your heart and with all your soul and with all your mind and with all your strength.'
31 "The second is this: 'Love your neighbor as yourself.' There is no commandment greater than these."

GENESIS 1:27

27 So God created mankind in His own image, in the image of God he created them; male and female he created them.

Jesus shares the same emotions as us. He celebrates with us, and He mourns with us.

He took on all of our pain and suffering as He died on the cross for us. He loved us THAT much! He knew there was no other way, so He sacrificed His own life so that we might choose to walk with Him on a daily basis and share life with Him. He knows the temptations we face and how hard life can get, that's why He sits at the right hand of the Father and prays for us. You are always on His mind.

Sometimes we can feel stuck because we keep making the same mistakes, we keep giving into temptations and we might not even know why; we're just used to it, it's normal. Well, if we don't adjust our thought process, then what is really going to change?

Maybe we just need to recognize in a given situation, "Whoa, I'm being tempted right now." Start by acknowledging the fact that this happens and then ask yourself, "What robs my love for Jesus? How can I bring Jesus into these areas of my life?"

SWIMMING IN A POOL OF BAD DREAMS

EVERYWHERE I GO, EVERYWHERE I'VE BEEN,
I'M SWIMMING IN A POOL OF BAD DREAMS.
EVERYTHING I SAY, EVERYTHING I DO,
I'M DROWNING IN A POOL OF BAD THINGS.

WOE IS ME.

THIS GUILT DRIPS DOWN MY CHEEKS
EVERY TIME I HEAR YOU SPEAK.
I FALL DOWN & YOU PICK ME UP FROM BENT KNEES.

IT'S CALM, IT'S GENTLE, IT'S LOVE, IT'S SENTIMENTAL.
IT'S FREEDOM, IT'S FORGIVIN', IT'S HOPE; THIS IS LIVIN'.

THIS GUILT DRIPS DOWN MY CHEEKS
EVERY TIME I HEAR YOU SPEAK.
I FALL DOWN & YOU PICK ME UP FROM BENT KNEES.

MY FAILURE BRINGS YOUR SUCCESS.
MY ABANDONMENT BRINGS YOUR WARM-HEARTEDNESS.
MY WEAKNESS BRINGS YOUR STRENGTH,
& IT'S ALL OF THIS WE PRAY, IN JESUS' NAME.

HEBREWS 4:14-16

14 Therefore, since we have a great high priest who has ascended into heaven, Jesus the Son of God, let us hold firmly to the faith we profess. **15** For we do not have a high priest who is unable to empathize with our weaknesses, but we have one who has been tempted in every way, just as we are - yet he did not sin. **16** Let us then approach God's throne of grace with confidence, so that we may receive mercy and find grace to help us in our time of need.

2 CORINTHIANS 12:10

10 That is why, for Christ's sake, I delight in weaknesses, in insults, in hardships, in persecutions, in difficulties. For when I am weak then I am strong.

1 PETER 1:6-8

6 In all this you greatly rejoice, though now for a little while you may have had to suffer grief in all kinds of trials. **7** These have come so that the proven genuineness of your faith... may result in praise, glory and honor when Jesus Christ is revealed. **8** Though you have not seen him, you love him; and even though you do not see him now, you believe in him and are filled with an inexpressible and glorious joy...

In our most vulnerable moments, our weakest feelings, our lowest lows, we are able to experience the wonders of God's healing abilities IF we give Him the chance.

Stretch out your arms—create a metaphorical basket. Put your hurt in there; put your sin in there, your failing relationships, your broken homes, your doubt, your mis-trust, your abuse, and throw it up to God. "Take this from me, God! I need your love right now. I need your hand to lead me through this battle, this guilt, this pain, all of which is temporary, I know, but it hurts. Please, God, lift me up so I can experience Your mercy and Your grace, which you abundantly have to offer. Speak some sense of direction into my life as you spoke this world into existence. I'm ready for something more, and I believe You can sustain me."

SPIRITUALLY FED

SPIRITUALLY FED & NO LONGER THIRSTY,
YET I CAN CONTINUE TO EAT & SEEK FIRST THEE.

THE LORD FILLS ME UP AS I CONTINUE TO BELIEVE,
A SELF-LESS RESPONSE DEMONSTRATED TO ME.
THE RIM OF MY CUP IS BUT UH GLIMPSE OF HIS LOVE;
HOW IT SPILLS OVER THE LIP, I CAN'T THANK HIM ENOUGH.

ALPHA & OMEGA, EVER-PRESENT & ALL-KNOWING;
THE RIVERS OF LIVING WATER ARE GUSHING & OVERFLOWING.

WAVES OF MERCY & GRACE ARE DISPLACED ON THE SHORELINE
OF MY SOUL.
ERODING THE CORROSIVE CHARACTERISTICS, OF THIS,
INGLORIOUS TROLL.
THE SEARCH IS OVER AT LAST;
JESUS, YOU ARE THE SAND IN MY GLASS.

IN & OUT OF THE FURNACE;
THIS LIFE IS A TEMPORARY FLASH.
HELL ON EARTH AS FAR AS I'M CONCERNED.
I NEED ALL THE HELP I CAN GET SO I DON'T FEEL THE ETERNAL BURN.

EXAMPLES OF YOUR TRUTH ARE OUTLINED IN YOUR SCRIPTURE.
PROMISES & PROOF OF YOUR EXISTENCE IS A FIXTURE,
TO FORM THE FOUNDATION & POUR THE PERFECT MIXTURE,
TO WITHSTAND THE STORM, THAT'S SURE TO BE DELIVERED.

JOHN 6:35

35 Then Jesus declared, "I am the bread of life. Whoever comes to me will never go hungry, and whoever believes in me will never be thirsty."

REVELATION 21:6-8

6 ..."It is done. I am the Alpha and the Omega, the Beginning and the End. To the thirsty I will give water without cost from the spring of the water of life. 7 Those who are victorious will inherit all this, and I will be their God and they will be my children. 8 But the cowardly, the unbelieving, the vile, the murderers, the sexually immoral, those who practice magic arts, the idolaters and all liars—they will be consigned to the fiery lake of burning sulfur. This is the second death."

JOHN 7:37-38

37 ...Jesus stood and said in a loud voice, "Let anyone who is thirsty come to me and drink. 38 Whoever believes in me, as Scripture has said, rivers of living water will flow from within them."

LUKE 6:47-49

47 "As for everyone who comes to me and hears my words and puts them into practice, I will show you what they are like. 48 They are like a man building a house, who dug down deep and laid the foundation on rock. When a flood came, the torrent struck that house but could not shake it, because it was well built. 49 But the one who hears my words and does not put them into practice is like a man who built a house on the ground without a foundation. The moment the torrent struck that house, it collapsed and its destruction was complete."

How wonderful is our God?! A living example of where we can put our hope and rely on sustainability. He saves us from the shipwrecks in our lives and restores us so mercifully. He accepts us as sick, broken, hurting children and nurtures us back to health. He is the one true God. The LORD of Lords, the KING of Kings. The only one who offers salvation... and we don't even deserve it. This is the definition of grace.

"For the wages of sin is death," and through Jesus we can have life (Romans 6:23).

How will you reflect God's mercy and grace today? Maybe it's a Holy Spirit–provoking act toward someone you know; maybe a stranger… Maybe it's a moment of basking in the gratitude of healing where God has been providing restoration…

Write these thoughts down, these feelings, and add a prayer of hopefulness or thanks to go along with them. God be with you on this day.

BURNT

BEEN SEASONING MY LIFE WITH THESE NEGATIVE FLAVORS.
I'M READY TO REPLACE THIS DISTASTE SO I CAN SAVOR
SOMETHING GREATER.

I'M EITHER ENGULFED IN THE FLAMES
OR GETTIN' SMOKED OUT BY THE RAINS;
FINDING THAT HAPPY MEDIUM JUST SEEMS RARE THESE DAYS.

MY TANK IS ON EMPTY, BUT IT'S FUELED WITH YOUR GAS.
SO I KNOW THE SPARK WILL BE PLENTY; I DON'T EVEN HAVE TO ASK.

I TURN THE KNOB & LET 'ER RIP;
THE SUNLIGHT HITS & SOMETHIN' STIRS WITHIN.
A FAITH REFORMS THIS COUNTER-CULTURE KID.

I FEEL LIKE I'M BEING RAKED OVER THE COALS
AS I SENSE THE SPIRIT BREAKING & ENTERING MY SOUL.
THIS REVEALING SLICE OF PARADISE IS SALTED WITH THE
SCATTERED ASH FORETOLD.

I NEED MORE THAN A TASTE, MORE THAN A SAMPLE.
I WANT TO MARINATE IN YOUR PRESENCE,
A HEAVENLY SCRAMBLE... I'MMA LET THAT SOAK IN...

LORD. YOU ARE THE MAIN INGREDIENT TO THE RECIPE OF LIFE.
YOUR GLORY RADIATES THRU MY SLIGHTLY CLOSED EYES;
THIS IS ME BEING TENDERIZED.

THE FEELING OF WARM SAND IS SURROUNDING ME EQUALLY.
I LET MYSELF RISE TO YOUR COMFORTING FREQUENCY.
THE FIXIN'S, 'N SIDE', THE FORGIVENESS OF MY DELINQUENCY.
THIS PEACEFUL HARMONY IS DEEPENING SO FREQUENTLY;
I CAN'T WAIT FOR ETERNITY.

UNTIL THEN, I GUESS I'M BURNT!

NAAAAA...

I GOT YOUR WORD FOR DISCRETION,
THE HOLY SPIRIT FOR DIRECTION,
& JESUS' REPRESENTATION
TO LEAVE A LONG-LASTING IMPRESSION.

& I THANK YOU.

GALATIANS 5:13, 17, 19-26

13 You, my brothers and sisters were called to be free. But do not use your freedoms to indulge the flesh; rather, serve one another humbly in love.
17 For the flesh desires what is contrary to the Spirit and the Spirit what is contrary to the flesh. They are in conflict with each other…
19 The acts of the flesh are obvious: sexual immorality, impurity and debauchery; **20** idolatry and witchcraft; hatred, discord, jealousy, fits of rage, selfish ambition, dissensions, factions **21** and envy; drunkenness, orgies, and the like. I warn you, as I did before, that those who live like this will not inherit the kingdom of God.
22 But the fruit of the Spirit is love, joy, peace, forbearance, kindness, goodness, faithfulness, **23** gentleness and self-control. Against such things there is no law.
24 Those who belong to Christ Jesus have crucified the flesh with its passions and desires. **25** Since we live by the Spirit, let us keep in step with the Spirit. **26** Let us not become conceited, provoking and envying each other.

2 PETER 3:7, 13

7 By the same word the present heavens and earth are reserved for fire, being kept for a day of judgement and destruction of the ungodly.
13 But in keeping with his promise we are looking forward to a new heaven and a new earth, where righteousness dwells.

Do you ever feel like you're being pulled in different directions? Well, you are. Okay, good, great, glad that's solved, right? Feel better? No, of course not. Truth is, every day, multiple times a day, we are wondering how to handle situations. Hopefully by now we're thinking before we speak and working on laying out short-term and long-term goals and asking ourselves, "Is this decision going to help me achieve my goals or interfere with my goals?" If we are at this point, then analyzing those goals/plans is next. "Why do I want to achieve this goal?" More importantly, "Is this idea coming from within my own desires, my own wants, to satisfy my own needs—the flesh? Or is this something really pressing on my heart? For the love and benefit of others?"

Basically, this is what we're all up against—a tug-of-war between the flesh and the heart. Thankfully, some of us will finally surrender ourselves to a softened heart, realizing we need help and we're tired of trying to pretend everything is okay. We've asked and trusted God to mold us and shape us into the person He wants us to be.

The multitude of unwanted consequences coming from our fleshly desires becomes too much to bear, and we can't even look at ourselves in the mirror. In fact, when we do, all we see is disappointment. Maybe you're here now, maybe you're not, but I'll tell you, as with everything else in this book, I'm speaking from my own personal experience. There has to be something better than this, and I have found that putting my hope in Jesus and relying on His mercy and grace is the only thing that truly satisfies my inner-most reason for being. Everything else is just fun, dangerous, or distracting.

So, what kind of seasonings are you sprinkling in your life?

What three achievements do you desire on a monthly timeline? What's motivating these monthly plans?

What three achievements do you desire on a three year timeline? What's motivating these plans?

Identify some of the distractions in your life. Explain how you will handle them in the future to prevent them from getting in the way of you achieving your goals.

COMPETITIVE ARROGANCE

COMPETITIVE ARROGANCE CREATES AN ADDICTIVE VIBRATION.
PRIDEFUL SATURATION BLEEDS A NARCISSISTIC INFLATION.
NOW I'M DROWNING IN A FLAWED REPRESENTATION OF GREATNESS
& MANIPULATION.

I'M OVERLY CONFIDENT, & IT'S CAUSE FOR CONCERN.
CHARGING THRU LIFE WITH NO APTITUDE TO SERVE.
CONCEITED & SMUG, THIS ACT MUST REVERSE.
SEEKING THE APPROVAL OF MORTAL HUMAN BEINGS HAS BECOME
SOMEWHAT OF A CURSE.

UPLOAD THE PHOTO, RE-SPEAK THE TWEET.
DISCOMBOBULATING THE TRUTH. GRIEVING. DECEIT.
SINCE WHEN HAS BEING ORIGINAL BECOME SO OBSOLETE?

HERE COMES THE CONTRADICTION; I'M CALLING MYSELF A SHEEP,
THE LORD IS MY SHEPHERD, & I'M READY TO EAT.
ALONE & ON MY KNEES, WITH MY TEAR-STAINED CHEEKS,
REALIZING MY PAIN, IS FROM SELF-SEEKING SCHEMES.
I'M READY TO CONFRONT. I'M READY TO REPENT.
I'M READY TO ACCEPT, THE SON YOU HAVE SENT.

LORD JESUS, IT SEEMS, YOU KNOW WHO I'VE BEEN,
LIVIN' LIFE IN THE SHADOWS, FIGHTING THESE BATTLES FROM WITHIN.
YOU COME DOWN FROM YOUR HIGH PLACE & BRING ME BACK IN
& AGAIN & AGAIN. I CAN'T STAND TO ADMIT,
THAT I'M SICK OF THE GUILT OF LIVING LIKE THIS.

PLEASE, LORD, FORGIVE ME OF MY SINS.
MY SELFISH WAYS, MY SELF-CENTERED DECISIONS.
I WANT TO BE MORE LIKE YOU.
PLEASE PUT THE LOVE FOR OTHERS BACK INTO MY HEART
& HELP ME TO SHARE OF YOUR FAITHFULNESS, WHICH I HAVE
EXPERIENCED THUS FAR.
I KNOW YOU CAN HEAR ME; I KNOW YOU WILL PROVIDE.
THANK YOU FOR YOUR SON JESUS
& THE PROMISE OF ETERNAL LIFE.

AMEN

I JOHN 5:11–15

11 And this is the testimony: God has given us eternal life, and this life is in his Son. Whoever has the Son has life; **12** whoever does not have the Son of God does not have life. **13** I write these things to you who believe in the name of the Son of God so that you may know that you have eternal life. **14** This is the confidence we have in approaching God: that if we ask anything according to his will, he hears us. **15** And if we know that he hears us—whatever we ask—we know that we have what we asked of him.

GALATIANS 1:10

10 Am I now trying to win the approval of human beings, or of God? Or am I trying to please people? If I were still trying to please people, I would not be a servant of Christ.

PSALM 100:3

3 Know that the LORD is God. It is he who made us, and we are his; we are his people, the sheep of his pasture.

JOHN 10:14–15

[Jesus says:] **14** "I am the good shepherd; I know my sheep and my sheep know me—**15** just as the Father knows me and I know the Father—and I lay down my life for sheep."

Let's face it; we're all cattle roaming around in some pasture or pen... Who is your shepherd? Is it your boss? Your job? Money in general? Video games? Maybe the sports world governs your schedule? Soccer? Football? Is it a substance that tells you how to live your life? Who or what is leading you through the day? Who is feeding you, and what are they feeding you?

Maybe you're the self-sustaining type and don't need help from anyone... Maybe you are or think you are the shepherd..., even shepherds gotta eat. Will you look to your sheep for provisions when you can no longer fend off the wolves by yourself? Where will your help come from when your shepherd becomes un-reliable?

I guarantee every earthly shepherd has faults. At some point you will be let down or worse, led astray. Some of us might already be fending for ourselves, and we're looking for a way to get back on the trail, so to speak. If you recognize this about yourself, there is hope for you. There is eternal hope with Jesus as your shepherd. He is calling your name. He wants to provide for you, now and forever.

Will you let Him?

UN-CHAINED

UN-CHAINED & UN-BROKEN.
SINCE THE DAWN OF CREATION,
I HAVE BEEN CHOSEN.
THIS TRANSFORMATION CAN'T GO UN-SPOKEN.

I DON'T KNOW WHY I TOOK SO LONG TO CHANGE,
ALWAYS WANTING TO FIT IN, BEING AFRAID.
WORRYING ABOUT BEING A CAST-OUT,
THEN WAKING UP, REALIZING I'D PASSED OUT...
THAT'S PUTTING IT LIGHTLY; NO DOUBT I WAS BLACKED OUT.
STILL FEELING LEFT OUT,
LIVING LIFE AS A BURNT OUT,
LOOKIN' AROUND LIKE, "WHO'S COUCH?" ... OUCH.

STRUGGLE ON, STRUGGLE OFF.
TROUBLE ONCE, DOUBLE LOSS.
FIGHTING THESE FEELINGS, THE URGE TO SUBMIT,
YOUR VOICE IN THE NIGHT; MY CONSCIENCE WON'T QUIT!

KNOWING WHAT'S RIGHT, STILL DOING WHAT'S WRONG,
THEN YOU COME BACK & GUIDE ME ALONG.
I PLEAD & I POUT.
I SCREAM & I SHOUT,
& WHEN IT'S ALL BETTER,
I GO RIGHT BACK OUT.

THE HUMILITY, THESE LESSONS,
THE NEED FOR CORRECTION...
MY LIFE IS NO SECRET;
IT'S PLANNED TO PERFECTION.

YOUR LOVE HASN'T CHANGED.
YOUR PATIENCE HAS AMAZED.
IN A WORLD FULL OF DARK,
YOUR LIGHT SHINES THE WAY.

No Longer Bound by CHAINS

LUKE 15:11-32

(Please read "The Parable of the Lost Son")
17 ... He came to his senses...

1 CORINTHIANS 15:33-34

33 Do not be misled: "Bad company corrupts good character." **34** Come back to your senses as you ought and stop sinning...

ECCLESIASTES 5:4

4 When you make a vow to God, do not delay to fulfill it.

PSALM 119:105

105 Your word is a lamp for my feet, a light on my path.

HEBREWS 12:7, 11

7 Endure hardship as discipline; God is treating you as his children. For what children are not disciplined by their father?
11 No discipline seems pleasant at the time, but painful. Later on, however, it produces a harvest of righteousness and peace for those who have been trained by it.

Can you remember a time (or two) where you made a promise to God, an oath and then broke that promise by not following through with your end of the deal? "I swear I'll change my ways if You get me out of this one!" Or, "This is the last time, I promise." Truth is, God knows you better than that. He knows you need help, and He knows certain doses of discipline are required.

Question is, how much discipline is it going to take for you to notice the consequent patterns in your life, and when are you (and God) going to work on preventing such situations from interfering with what God has in store for you? That's right, preventing consequences.

If every time I go out drinking, I get in a fight, I should probably quit going out drinking. If a pattern develops where I'm constantly asking other people for money, I might want to consider changing my spending habits. What am I doing to prevent tooth pain? What is preventing me from eating healthy? Taking care of my body?

Lots of our hurt is self-inflicted, and if we're willing to plead with God to get us out of situations to prevent pain and heartache, what's stopping us from pleading with God for some self-control and guidance to save us from the "discipline" before it happens? In the production and manufacturing industry, this is called "Total Preventative Maintenance" or TPM.

Even further, how great is it that in the midst of our pain, we can thank God for showing us His love as He interferes to bring on a pause in our actions, eliminating the possibility of further self-destruction? Chances are, if you're reading this, you've already identified some of these ideas, and I applaud you for your courageous desire to break the cycle.

What does your TPM report look like?

RE-ARRANGED BELIEF

RE-ARRANGED BELIEF, COMING IN BETWEEN,
THE ABSENT MINDED & THESE COMPETENT DREAMS,
& SO IT SEEMS, THAT THESE,
STRONG CONVICTIONS ARE LEADING ME
TO UP & LEAVE THE UN-FULFILLING NORMALCY.
THE 9-5 OR 6-3, WHATEVER IT MAY BE,
IS NO LONGER WORKING NATURALLY.

I'M PENT UP, IN A RAGE, TRAPPED IN THIS OFFICE CAGE.
SWIRLING THOUGHTS, CONFRONTATIONALLY STRANGE.
UNABLE TO MAKE DECISIONS WITHOUT THE SPIRITS INTERFERING
& SUGGESTING ALTERNATE WAYS.
JESUS, I NEED YOUR SPIRIT TO STAY.
REBUKE THE EVIL ONE; MAKE HIM GO AWAY.

I DON'T WANT TO FALL INTO SLAVERY WORKING FOR THE MAN,
FEELING SAFE ABOUT MY FINANCES;
I WANT TO BE A SLAVE TO YOUR HAND,
SECURE ABOUT MY ETERNAL CIRCUMSTANCES.

MY MIND IS ELSEWHERE, THIS IS EVIDENT;
FAITHFULLY LEANING ON YOUR BENEVOLENCE,
I REMAIN FOCUSED ON MY HEAVENLY INHERITANCE.

NOW I'M ON THIS POETIC PATH OF SELF-REFLECTION.
A JOURNEY THRU LIFE, BATTLING TRUTH & DECEPTION.
A COMPLEX ORIENTATION OF CHOICE & SELECTION;
PRAYING FOR STRAIGHT PATHS & SOME SENSE OF DIRECTION.
LOOKING FOR EXCITING WAYS TO ABSTAIN COMPLACENCY
WITHOUT LEADING MYSELF INTO DORMANT VACANCY.

I CAN'T CONTROL MY THOUGHTS,
BUT I CAN CONTROL WHAT I PUT INTO MY TIME SLOTS,
SO I'M FAITHFULLY LIVING OUT MY PURPOSE
BY LETTING THESE WORDS DROP.
SO, IF I CAN ENCOURAGE YOU TO STAY, REAL QUICK,
I'M GONNA PRAY:
LORD JESUS, THANK YOU FOR THIS DAY!
THANK YOU FOR ALL THAT YOU'RE DOING IN MY LIFE RIGHT NOW.
I CAN'T COMPLAIN,
'CAUSE I KNOW THAT YOU ARE WITH ME EVERY STEP OF THE WAY.
I ASK THAT YOU CONTINUE TO BE MY STRENGTH,
ESPECIALLY WHEN I AM WEAK, & PLEASE,
LOOK OUT FOR MY FAMILY & MY FRIENDS.

AMEN

PROVERBS 3:5-6

5 Trust in the LORD with all your heart and lean not on your own understanding; **6** in all your ways submit to him, and he will make your paths straight.

EPHESIANS 6:12

12 For our struggle is not against flesh and blood, but against the rulers, against the authorities, against the powers of this dark world and against the spiritual forces of evil in the heavenly realms.

ROMANS 8:14-17

14 For those who are led by the Spirit of God are the children of God. **15** The Spirit you received does not make you slaves, so that you live in fear again; rather, the Spirit you received brought about your adoption to sonship. And by Him we cry, "Abba Father." **16** The Spirit himself testifies with our spirit that we are God's children. **17** Now if we are children, then we are heirs—heirs of God and co-heirs with Christ, if indeed we share in His sufferings in order that we may also share in his glory.

Life is basically choice weighted with sacrifice. "What is more important and how much time do I have?" From the moment we wake up in the morning, we are deciding what to eat, what to wear, what to watch, what to read, what to do. Some decisions require more thought, and this is where we weigh out the positive and negative reasons for the choice.

For example, we may choose to go to work in the morning and skip breakfast because we don't have enough time because we chose to hit the snooze button too many times. Starting work on time is more important than a thought-out eating plan: breakfast, lunch, and dinner. If we typically prepare breakfast, then this example would be a reaction to the time constraint. A reaction is commonly impulsive and negative, maybe even irrational, with little thought going into the decision. The obvious response to this example is to wake up when our alarm goes off, allowing enough time to prepare breakfast AND make it to work on time; no need for sacrifice or prioritizing one thing over the other, i.e., starting work on time or eating breakfast.

Responding to life is positive. Think about what's coming and prepare yourself. "Do I continue to bring home a negative attitude and bitterness towards other people or do I allow a spiritual intervention to promote a positive response to my situational struggles and shortcomings? Will I continue to rely on other people to solve my problems, or is it time to develop a faith I can rely on to find comfort in challenging times of uncertainty? I can keep battling these emotional hardships, or I can read my Bible and learn about God's love for me and better understand how to live out my purpose."

Stop reacting to life and start responding to life.

Breakfast is simple. Snacks, fast food, and lunch are right around the corner.

Death? Maybe not so simple, and eternity is a whole lotta time.

Make a deal with yourself right now and agree to replace a reaction with a response from your daily routine. Ask God to help prepare your thoughts, your tongue, your judgment, your focus, etc., for whatever needs the discipline.

GIVE IT ALL

PIECEMEAL' RECOVERY.
PSYCHOLOGICAL DISCOVERY.
ANOTHER SNAP-SHOT OF TIME-LAPSE,
RE-FRAMING MY PSYCHĒ.

I'M A CLOSE-UP PHOTOGRAPHER WITH A BIG-PICTURE FOCUS,
I KNOW THIS;
AN INDECISIVE, MICRO-DOSIN', MACRO-SCŌPIC GERM.
LOOKIN' AT LIFE WITH DISTORTED CORNEA & APERTURE TO BURN,
ADJUSTING MY SIGHT TO LET IN MORE LIGHT
SO I CAN SEE CLEARLY ALL THERE IS YOU WANT ME TO LEARN.

I'M DONE BEING THE DIRECTOR.
I'VE FAILED AT BEING THE PRODUCER.
& GOD'S BLESSINGS DONE STITCHED ME UP LIKE A SUTURE,
SO I AIN'T GONNA FEAR NO FUTURE!
'CAUSE FOR ONCE HE'S GOT THE LEAD ROLE, THE MAIN PART.
I'M GONNA COURAGEOUSLY DO WHAT I'M TOLD AS HE SOFTENS MY
CALLOUSED HEART.
THIS FILM CAN ONLY BE DEVELOPED FROM ABOVE,
FORGIVE & FORGET, NOW THAT'S TRUE LOVE.

THE LORD KEEPS NO RECORD OF WRONGS;
YOU CAN TAKE THAT TO THE BANK,
OR IN JESUS' CASE,
HE TOOK IT STRAIGHT TO HIS PALMS.

THANK YOU FOR YOUR FORGIVENESS,
WHICH WE KNOW'S IN HIGH DEMAND;
NOT FOR SECOND AM I EXPECTIN'
MY HUMAN PROBLEMS
TO BE SOLVED WITH HUMAN HANDS.
I CAN'T EVEN BEGIN TO EXPLAIN HOW GRATEFUL I AM,
THAT YOU WOULD FIND FAVOR IN THIS SINFUL MAN.

SO I GIVE IT ALL TO YOU.
EVERY LAST BIT.
MY PRIVATE & MY PUBLIC CONFLICT.

I DON'T WANNA FEED YOU LOST & EMPTY WORDS,
SO I'M LETTIN' YOU DRAW UP THE STORYBOARD,
I'LL LET MY FAITH PRODUCE THE WORKS.

JESUS, I LOVE YOU.

1 JOHN 4:8

8 Whoever does not love does not know God, because God is love.

1 CORINTHIANS 13:4-7

4 Love is patient, love is kind. It does not envy, it does not boast, it is not proud. 5 It does not dishonor others, it is not self-seeking, it is not easily angered, it keeps no record of wrongs. 6 Love does not delight in evil but rejoices with the truth. 7 It always protects, always trusts, always hopes, always perseveres.

JAMES 2:17, 26

17 In the same way, faith by itself, if it is not accompanied by action, is dead. 26 As the body without the spirit is dead, so faith without deeds is dead.

EPHESIANS 2:8-10

8 For it is by grace you have been saved, through faith—and this is not from yourselves, it is the gift of God 9 not by works, so that no one can boast. 10 For we are God's handiwork, created in Christ Jesus to do good works, which God prepared in advance for us to do.

1 JOHN 3:18

18 Dear children, let us not love with words or speech but with actions and in truth.

Let's be clear; our actions, our works, our deeds will NOT get us into Heaven. We can't earn a spot or beat out somebody else. It's not a point system. We are not able to save ourselves. By God's grace alone we have been saved.

Our faith in God and believing in the resurrection of His son Jesus Christ leads us into wanting to serve. Once we begin to understand the love He has for us, the sacrifice He has made for us, we want to become more like Him. We want to learn more. We want to deepen our relationship with Him. Our hearts desire living out His purpose, which He reveals to us in small doses, one step at a time. "We love [Him] because He first loved us" (1 John 4:19). We show Him we love Him through our actions.

Today, SHOW someone they are loved, that they are cared for.

Make someone feel noticed, and this will be pleasing to God.

KEEP DREAMIN'

KEEP DREAMIN'. KEEP LEANIN',
IN FOR A CLOSER LOOK;
INSTRUCTIONS YIELDED FROM THE PAGES OF HIS BOOK.
RELAX.
THE PAST IS JACKED!
DON'T LET YOUR FUTURE DAYS RESEMBLE THAT.

OLD HABITS WILL DIE OFF.
OPEN WOUNDS WILL HEAL BACK,
I PROMISE.

LOOK FORWARD, PUSH PROGRESS,
LEAP HURDLES, BINGE-WATCH AS,
THIS TRANSFORMATION GETS PROCESSED.

MY HEART REJOICES AT THE MAGNITUDE OF YOUR MARVEL;
IT'S REMARKABLE!
A PRAISEWORTHY KING, A WARRIOR, THE VICTOR;
IMMEASURABLE BEAUTY, BOUNCING OFF THE RICHTER.

NO SCALE CAN CARRY THE WEIGHT OF MY SIN,
SO YOU SENT JESUS TO DIE & RISE AGAIN;
TO OFFSET THE IMBALANCE & BRING ME BACK IN.

MY LOPSIDED LIFE HAS BEEN TRANSFORMED BY YOUR GRACE.
MY INABILITY TO COMPREHEND HAS FINALLY SLAPPED ME IN THE FACE.
"AWAKE!"
THIS SLEEPER' GOT HIS FEET ON THE FLOOR. HE'S RUNNING OUT
THE DOOR;
HE'S CHARGING AGAINST THE INVALID LIE;
THIS AIN'T NO GAME—THIS IS WAR!

You've given me the power; I'm stronger than before.
You've pulled me out of hiding, suffering no more.

The darkest of valleys, the deepest of holes,
is now a relic of the past as Your arm reaches down
& Your hand grabs 'hold.

EPHESIANS 6:10-11, 14-17

10 Finally, be strong in the Lord and in His mighty power. **11** Put on the full armor of God, so that you can take your stand against the devil's schemes. **14** Stand firm then, with the belt of truth buckled around your waist, with the breastplate of righteousness in place, **15** and with your feet fitted with the readiness that comes from the gospel of peace **16** ... take up the shield of faith, with which you can extinguish all the flaming arrows of the evil one. **17** Take the helmet of salvation and the sword of the Spirit, which is the word of God.

EPHESIANS 5:14

14 ... "Wake up, sleeper, rise from the dead, and Christ will shine on you."

PSALM 18:6, 16-19, 27-28, 30, 32, 36, 46

6 In my distress I called to the LORD; I cried to my God for help. From his temple he heard my voice; my cry came before him, into his ears.

16 He reached down on high and took hold of me; he drew me out of deep waters.

17 He rescued me from my powerful enemy, from my foes, who were too strong for me.

18 They confronted me in the day of my disaster, but the LORD was my support.

19 He brought me out into a spacious place; he rescued me because he delighted in me.

27 You save the humble.

28 ... my God turns my darkness into light.

30 As for God, his way is perfect: The LORD's word is flawless; he shields all who take refuge in him.

32 It is God who arms me with strength and keeps my way secure.

36 You provide a broad path for my feet, so that my ankles do not give way.

46 The LORD lives! Praise be to my Rock! Exalted be God my Savior!

What a relief to know that we are not alone. That we are loved by our divine creator. That we, as believers, have the power of God living inside of us and all we have to do to activate this power is to humbly call out His name and admit we cannot do it on our own. Nor do we want to do it on our own (the "it" being life, choices, careers, relationships, hardships, etc.).

When I carry on in my own behavior by doing and saying what I think is best, I get in a world of trouble mentally, physically, financially... I absolutely need a savior. There's no way I'm going to make things better on my own. You feel me?

When I begin a dialogue with Christ, my hope is restored, and I'm inspired to keep seeking a better way. I don't have to stay stuck in this rut, feeling sorry for myself. I don't have to stay weak and feeble-minded, going into uncomfortable situations, i.e., courtrooms, P.O. offices, job interviews, in-laws, etc. I can be confident in my calling, knowing Jesus is with me, building me up courageously, shaping me according to my specific design and the unique journey He has me on. You are unique and special too! One of a kind, and God also wants to save you, no matter what your past looks like.

Make a choice today to repent of a sin, whatever that is, something that's bugging you. Turn away from this sin; stop engaging in it. The Bible says, "Resist the devil and he will flee from you" (James 4:7). Stop giving this sin your attention. You know what it is. Write it down. Pray for God's deliverance over this area. Eventually this sin will become a distant memory.

I wanna be real with ya; you're gonna have to work at it. Let me ask you, if you don't work at something and push yourself, is it really that important to you?

How important is your love for others?

How important is God's love to you?

How important is your salvation?

What does this even mean to you?

WHEN I JUST LET YOU

WHEN I JUST LET YOU, THE ME GETS A BREAK.
PHYSICAL, MENTAL, & EMOTIONAL ESCAPE.

WHEN I JUST LET YOU, THE ME CAN BREATHE.
SATURATED PEACE, SECURELY FREE.

WHEN I JUST LET YOU, THE ME IS RELAXED.
NO LONGER ATTACHED, NOT UNDER ATTACK.

WHEN I JUST LET YOU, THE ME CAN HEAR.
A WHISPER, A VOICE, YOUR SPIRIT IS NEAR.

WHEN I JUST LET YOU, THE ME SEES TRUE,
PROMISES BEING KEPT, FULFILLMENT IN PLAIN VIEW.

PSALM 119:37

37 Turn my eyes away from worthless things; preserve my life according to your word.

ECCLESIASTES 3:1–8

1 There is a time for everything, and a season for every activity under the heavens: **2** a time to be born and a time to die, a time to plant and a time to uproot, **3** a time to kill and a time to heal, a time to tear down and a time to build, **4** a time to weep and a time to laugh, a time to mourn and a time to dance, **5** a time to scatter stones and a time to gather them, a time to embrace and a time to refrain from embracing, **6** a time to search and a time to give up, a time to keep and a time to throw away, **7** a time to tear and a time to mend, a time to be silent and a time to speak, **8** a time to love and a time to hate, a time for war and a time for peace.

PSALM 16:11

11 You make known to me the path of life; you will fill me with joy in your presence, with eternal pleasures at your right hand.

Life is demanding. It's easy to get overwhelmed with everything that needs to get done. There's the stuff we have to do. The stuff we want to do, plus the stuff other people want us to do. All of this picking and choosing and what's important and time frames and schedules and worrying about how it's all going to get done before different deadlines and expectations and, and, and… Yes, this is the modern world. In the midst of all this, where are you finding your peace? Where is your relaxation station? How do you escape? Really… how are you coping with reality when stuff piles up on you? Take time to get honest with yourself about this part. What do your answers reveal about yourself?

Most of our hiding places are temporary and actually create even more stress and anxiety because we merely hit the pause button and delay resolution. After identifying what really is important and what really needs attention, ask yourself, "Do I really have control over the outcome of this situation or is this something I can trust God to work out?" Think about it and give God one or two things right now. For today. For this week. Maybe it's an upcoming meeting, or a phone call, or other type of conversation. Maybe you're dealing with transportation issues or babysitting issues. Whatever it is, have faith, be still, and know that you don't have to do it all on your own.

WAYS OF THE WORLD

THE WAYS OF THE WORLD GOT ME STUCK.
NEGATIVE FREQUENCIES, CONTROLLED, CORRUPT.
HOPELESS DISCOURAGEMENT, SUGARY JUNK.

ELECTRO-MAGNETIC BRAIN WAVE SIGNALING,
CONSTANT CORRECTION FOR THIS SLAVE-WAY IMAGING.

RUMINATION INVASION OF THESE MADE-UP CONVERSATIONS;
CAN'T SLEEP, LOST DREAMS, IRRITABLE VEGETATION.

WHY MUST I BEG? WHY MUST I PLEAD?
YOU KNOW THE DEPTHS OF MY HEART, HELP ME TO SEE;
THE WHATEVER IT IS, THE WHO I'M S'POSED TO BE,
THE HOW IT PLAYS OUT, STEPS 1, 2, & 3.

BREAK THESE CHAINS, THESE DAMAGING WAYS.
HELP ME TO "NOT PAY ATTENTION TO EVERY WORD PEOPLE SAY."
IT'S KILLING ME TO COMPLAIN;
THE TORTURE I SUSTAIN IS DRIVING ME INSANE.

I'M GUIDED TO YOUR WORD, THE TRUTH REVEALED TODAY:
"DO NOT LET YOUR HEARTS BE TROUBLED; DO NOT BE AFRAID."

PRAYERS WILL BE ANSWERED, THRU FAITH, GOD WILLING.
FOR HEALING AND HOPE GIVING, WILL YIELD,
A FEELING OF STOKED LIVING.

AMEN

JOHN 14:27

27 "Peace I leave with you; my peace I give you. I do not give to you
as the world gives.
Do not let your hearts be troubled and do not be afraid."

ECCLESIASTES 7:21

21 Do not pay attention to every word people say…

JOHN 15:19

19 "… As it is, you do not belong to the world, but I have chosen you
out of the world."

Do you know what Jesus has planned for your life? If you don't know, ask
him today with your words, with your heart. Write down these revelations,
these ideas, these inspirations, and continue to pray for guidance in
these areas. Ask Him to remove specific distractions and ask Him with a
convincing heart, knowing He will give you the answers.

How is human influence interfering with what Jesus has planned for
your life? What are you willing to do about that? What are you willing
to let God do about that?

Turn the news off a couple times a week. Stop engaging in what the
world has to offer. Stop relying on the public school systems to raise
your kids. Get involved in your community. Get off the couch and get
moving in a direction of serving. Show God you are ready to make a
difference. Too many of us think that a miracle is just going to fall into
our laps but no, you are the miracle, go and give away the hope that is
in you. Share the love of Jesus with someone.

Re-read John 15:19. Jesus says, "You do not belong to the world. I have
chosen you out of it." He wants so badly for you to understand there
is so much more in store for you. Jesus' intentions for your life go
far beyond your current state. Heaven, yes, for sure; don't wait until
Heaven, though. Start the experience today.

Continuous improvement. Continuous communication with Jesus.

STUCK IN THIS MAZE

STUCK IN THIS MAZE.
CAUGHT UP IN THIS RACE.
PRAYIN' FOR THE REVELATION
OF YOUR AMAZING GRACE;
HOW SWEET THE SOUND.
A FOOLISH CLOWN, LIVIN' ON BROKEN GROUND,
YET YOU CAN STILL LOOK DOWN & BE PROUD,
OF ME.

SUPERFLUOUS LOVE STRETCHING,
RADIANT SUN BEAMS OVER THE LOST & FOUND BEINGS.
THE UNDESERVING HUMAN RACE.
OUR POSITIVE HOPE IS YOUR NEGATIVE SPACE.

AS THEY FLOAT AROUND UP THERE IN THAT STATION,
IMPATIENTLY DENYING ALL OF YOUR CREATION,
SENDING BACK SIGNALS OF FALSE HOPES,
NOT PRAYING—
UN-COMPREHENSIVE, ASTRONOMICAL EXPLAINING.
WANTING US TO BELIEVE THERE'S NO YOU & NO SON—
LIFE BEGAN WITH THAT COSMIC EXPLOSION!
WORMHOLE & BLACK HOLE SEDUCTION!
MASS APPEAL FOR FAKE BELIEVIN'.
HIDE YOUR FEELINGS FROM THE FLOOR TO THE GLASS CEILIN'.
BLIND OUR EYES WITH WHAT THEY WANT US TO BE SEEIN'.
IT'S ALL A LIE;
IT'S GOT ME SCREAMIN'!
I'M FUMIN'!
EXPLODING CLOUDS OF SMOKE PLUMIN'!
LIKE THE SPACESHIPS AT LIFT-OFF,

ROCKET BOOSTERS BOOMIN'!
THEN UP, UP, & AWAY, BUT WAIT!
WHY IS THIS THING GOIN' SIDEWAYS?
THIS AIN'T THE WAY TO SPACE; THIS MUST BE SOME MISTAKE!
NA$A SHOUTS HOORAY AS THE SHUTTLE FLIES FARTHER AWAY.
THE HOLLYWOOD CROWD CELEBRATES & STANDS PROUD.
YOU HEAR THE 'OOOHS' & 'AHHS'; IT'S A MILLION-DOLLAR FACADE!

THE TAX MAN COLLECTS ON CIVILIAN NEGLECT.
POWER TO THE ELITE WHILE THE SICK DIE IN THE STREET.
EVIL DOESN'T SLEEP,
& THAT'S WHY WE NEED YOUR PROMISES ON REPEAT.

MATTHEW 28:20

20 "... I [Jesus] am with you always, to the very end of the age."

2 CORINTHIANS 1:20

20 For no matter how many promises God has made, they are "Yes" in Christ.

JOHN 11:25–26

25 Jesus said to her, "I am the resurrection and the life.
The one who believes in me will live,
even though they die; 26 and whoever lives by believing in me will never die..."

ISAIAH 54:10

10 "Though the mountains be shaken and the hills be removed, yet my unfailing love for you will not be shaken nor my covenant of peace be removed," says the LORD, who has compassion on you.

ISAIAH 32:7

7 Scoundrels use wicked methods, they make up evil schemes to destroy the poor with lies. Even when the plea of the needy is just.

These are just a few promises from God's word, and the main idea here is pretty simple: God is on our side. He sees our every move. He knows our every thought. He tests the heart, our motives. He is a God of justice.

The false prophets/teachers, the ones who use their power to deceive and manipulate— best believe they're gonna get it the worst; it's not our place to decide their penalties or get in the way of God's wrath. God is in control of everything! Let's let God be God and let us cast our sorrows, our pain, our fears to Him. Let Him use our negative feelings and our negative thoughts for good. He is the restorer of hope. The evildoers, the wicked schemers—God will handle them accordingly (Romans 2:6-8).

When we focus and invest time in all of the negativity, guess what? We become more negative and un-certain. When we focus on God's love, God's peace, and God's promises, we will be content with His presence and confident in our restoration. His light will shine through us into this dark world.

Write down a few of your favorite promises that God has made and thank Him for these promises in prayer. Open your eyes to His truths and share His story of victory. Let's not dwell in confusion or excite in playing the victim card. Let's stop looking for ways to be offended, and let us delight in how we overcome adversity.

God is with you.

MY SOLITUDE

MY SOLITUDE, YOUR VOICE.
MY BREATHING, YOUR CHOICE.
TIME HAS NO ESSENCE
WHEN DEALING WITH YOUR PRESENCE.
LIQUEFACTION OF PLASMA,
WHERE BALLS OF LIGHT GATHER.
A GLEAMING ARRAY OF WONDER,
A RADIANT LAPSE OF SUMMER.
THIS FEELING, THIS MOMENT,
THIS SPELL THAT I AM UNDER.
A 360° VIEW
OF YOUR TRIED & TRUE;
CREATION, EXISTENCE,
ALL ON YOUR CUE.
FLOATING, QUOTING,
SUPERNATURAL SCRIPTURE.
LISTENING, AGAINST THIS,
HORIZONTAL PICTURE.
IT'S HAPPENING, THE BEAUTY,
FROM THIS, SELECTION.
THE GATHERING, THE UNITY,
THE ONENESS, PERFECTION.
REMARKABLE SATISFACTION,
ME & YOU.
UNSHAKABLE ATTRACTION,
SINCE MY MOTHER'S WOMB.
RELAXED, CALM, MEDITATED, & JUST.
SURPASSED, ALL, DEDICATED, YOU MUST.

PHILIPPIANS 4:8

8 Finally, brothers and sisters, whatever is true, whatever is noble, whatever is right, whatever is pure, whatever is lovely, whatever is admirable—if anything is excellent or praiseworthy—think about such things.

PSALM 139:13–14

13 For you created my inmost being; you knit me together in my mother's womb.
14 I praise you because I am fearfully and wonderfully made; Your works are wonderful, I know that full well.

HEBREWS 11:3

3 By faith we understand that the universe was formed at God's command, so that what is seen was not made out of what was visible.

Stay positive. Stay calm. We are surrounded by God's love, by His beauty. Give Him praise in all things; For wherever you go, there you are, and He is with you… Since the very beginning, He has had a plan for you. Be confident in your hope for a quiet place where His voice will be revealed to you.

SELF-REFLECTION

SELF-REFLECTION, DOESN'T EQUAL MUCH.

LOVE CONNECTION, YOUR SECRET TRUST.

MIS-DIRECTION, LOST WITH A BAD CRUTCH.

TRUE AFFECTION, FIXING ALL THIS BROKEN STUFF.

FLESH COMPLEXION, NEVER BEEN THAT TOUGH.

JESUS' RESURRECTION, HAS ALWAYS BEEN ENOUGH.

JOHN 3:16

16 For God so loved the world that he gave his one and only Son, that whoever believes in him shall not perish but have eternal life.

MATTHEW 28:6

6 "...he has risen, just as he said..."

1 PETER 1:3-4

3 ... In his great mercy he has given us new birth into a living hope through the resurrection of Jesus Christ from the dead, **4** and into an inheritance that can never perish, spoil or fade. This inheritance is kept in heaven for you...

If Jesus doesn't rise from the dead, this is all for nothing. We live complicated lives; we go around comparing ourselves with one another, seeking our own pleasures, and pretending to be something we're not just to feel accepted. When in reality, we were made from love [who is God], to be loved, and to share this love with God for eternity in Heaven.

If you believe in your heart and confess with your mouth, "Yes, Jesus did die for my sins, and yes, He did rise from the dead on my behalf so that I would have everlasting life with Him," then brother, sister, I will see you in Heaven!

Walk in this peace today. Walk in this promise. Remind yourself that Jesus rose from the dead for YOU and in everything, give thanks!

WALK WITH ME

WALK... WITH ME... THRU THE AGES OF TIME.
TURN... WITH ME... THRU THE PAGES OF LIFE.
I LONG... TO BE... IN YOUR RADIANT LIGHT.
AT THE FEET... OF JESUS... AT YOUR... RIGHT SIDE.
OH LORD... MY GOD... IT'S PLAIN TO SEE.
YOUR LOVE... YOUR MERCY... HAS SET... ME FREE.

YOUR WORDS ARE TRUE, MY LIFE APPROVED.
MY SIN, MY SHAME, ALL WASHED AWAY.
MY YOUTH RESTORED, MY SOUL BRAND NEW.
THIS WORSHIP, THIS PRAISE, IS ALL FOR YOU.

HE'S SEEN ME WORKIN'.
HE'S BEEN OBSERVANT.
HE CALLED UPON ME,
HIS FAITHFUL SERVANT.

HIS VOICE, I KNOW.
HIS FACE, NOW SHOWN.
AT LAST, RESIDE,
IN PARADISE.

WALK... WITH ME... THRU THE AGES OF TIME.
TURN... WITH ME... THRU THE PAGES OF LIFE.
I LONG... TO BE... IN YOUR RADIANT LIGHT.
AT THE FEET... OF JESUS... AT YOUR... RIGHT SIDE.
OH LORD... MY GOD... IT'S PLAIN TO SEE.
YOUR LOVE... YOUR MERCY... HAS SET... ME FREE.

HEBREWS 4:13

13 Nothing in all creation is hidden from God's sight. Everything is uncovered and laid bare before the eyes of him whom we must give account.

1 JOHN 1:9

9 If we confess our sins, he is faithful and just and will forgive us our sins and purify us from all unrighteousness.

ROMANS 14:8, 10–12

8 If we live, we live for the Lord; and if we die, we die for the Lord. **10** ...For we will all stand before God's judgement seat. **11** It is written: "'As surely as I live,' says the Lord, 'every knee will bow before me; every tongue will acknowledge God.'" - ISAIAH 45:23
12 So then, each of us will give an account of ourselves to God.

For followers of Christ and believers of His message, the Gospel, we long for this opportunity to be with God.

Remember, He is faithful and merciful... and He wants a relationship with you so He can spoil you with His un-conditional love. The closer you're walking with God, the more involved He is in your life, the more you will be able to live the way He designed you to live.

What will the account of your life look like when you pass on? Will God recognize you as a faithful servant? When God asks, "What have you done with my son Jesus?" What will your answer be?

"...The LORD does not look at the things people look at.
People look at the outward appearance, but the LORD looks at the heart."

1 Samuel 16:7

CONCLUSION

SO IN CONCLUSION, I WRITE,
PRAYING THE DISILLUSION JUST MIGHT,
FADE FROM THE PRECEPTS OF DARKNESS,
INTO YOUR GLORIOUS LIGHT.

NO MORE SHADOW PUPPETS,
NO MORE BLIND LEADING THE BLIND.
NO MORE ROUGHIN' IT;
NO MORE GRIME SEIZING MY TIME.

ON THIS WALK OF REPENTANCE,
ASKING THAT THIS "CUP" BE WASHED
AND RINSED WITH FORGIVENESS...
SO THAT MY WORDS BRING YOU PRAISE
WITH EVERY SINGLE SENTENCE.

THANK YOU FOR JOINING ME ON THIS JOURNEY RIGHT HERE;
THIS TANGLED-UP MESS, A FRAYED LOOP OF STRESS,
CUTTING OFF THE SPLIT ENDS WITH SHEARS;
YOU'VE HELPED TO UNRAVEL THE STRANGER IN THE MIRROR...

HOW FAR WILL YOU TRAVEL IN HIS LIGHT THIS YEAR?

MATTHEW 23:23-26

23 "Woe to you, teachers of the law and Pharisees, you hypocrites! You give a tenth of your spices—mint, dill, and cumin. But you have neglected the more important matters of the law— justice, mercy and faithfulness. You should have practiced the latter without neglecting the former. **24** You blind guides! ... **25** Woe to you, teachers of the law and Pharisees, you hypocrites! You clean the outside of the cup and dish, but inside they are full of greed and self-indulgence. **26** Blind Pharisee! First clean the inside of the cup and dish, and then the outside also will be clean."

JOHN 11:47-53

47 Then the chief priests and the Pharisees called a meeting of the Sanhedrin... "Here is this man performing many signs. **48** If we let him go on like this, everyone will believe in him, and then the Romans will come and take away both our temple and our nation." **49** Then one of them, named Caiaphas, who was high priest that year, spoke up. "You know nothing at all! **50** You do not realize that it is better for you that one man die for the people than that the whole nation perish." **51** He did not say this on his own, but as high priest that year he prophesied that Jesus would die for the Jewish nation, **52** and not only for that nation but also for the scattered children of God, to bring them together and make them one. **53** So from that day on they plotted to take his life.

JOHN 12:9-11

9 Meanwhile a large crowd of Jews found out that Jesus was there and came, not only because of him but also to see Lazarus, whom he had raised from the dead. **10** So the chief priests made plans to kill Lazarus as well, **11** for on account of him many of the Jews were going over to Jesus and believing in him.

Believing in Jesus interferes with the created culture's power, the elite, and the governing officials... Since Jesus's time, even the religious officials wanted to intervene. In fact, they are the ones that started the discussion of being intimidated by His power:
Too many people are believing in Him - John 11:48.

They were discouraged so much, they wanted to kill Him, as verse 53 says.

Covering up and denying Jesus has been embedded in our culture for two thousand years! The progressive stance has compounded on itself... just look around. We are at war with a super-monster of a culture, whose only mission is to distract and separate us from any and all inclination of the existence of Jesus Christ—conditioning our mind, numbing our emotions, and normalizing sin.

As artificial intelligence locks its momentum into yet another foothold on the wall that's being built around our hearts, we can only expect the dissatisfaction of our society and the power of controlled, persuaded thinking to climb higher and higher—leaping over boundary lines, crushing moral standards.

The testing and the roll out of all this fingerprint and [partial] facial recognition is limited to our outward appearance. This collection of information only reveals distinguishable marks and the "what" we have done from an outside perspective. Only you and God know the "why" you have done and understand the motivation behind it.

Surveillance tech discriminates against these internal qualities because of its limited capacity; it's artificial, mind you. God, however, knows no limits. He will knock down every wall that gets in between Him and His children. He is fighting for you, and He will never give up. HallelujAH...

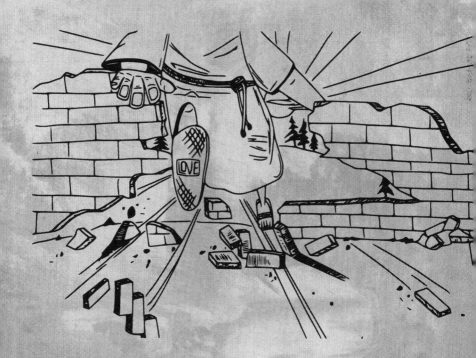

Then Jesus said, "Did I not tell you that if you believe, you will see the glory of God?"

John 11:40

Scripture Index

Old Testament

Genesis
1:27
2:7

Exodus
4:10–12
6:30
12:37

Deuteronomy
18:10–11

1 Samuel
16:7

Job
33:4

Psalm
16:11
18:6, 16–19, 27–28,
30, 32, 36, 46
43:1
46:10
56:3–4
100:3
116:1–2
119:37, 105
139:13–14

Proverbs
3:5–6

Ecclesiastes
3:1–8
5:4
7:21

Isaiah
30:21
32:7
45:23
49:15–16
54:10

Jeremiah
29:11, 12–14
31:34

Ezekiel
18:30–32

Habakuk
2:4

New Testament

Matthew
6:11, 19–31, 34
8:23–27
9:12–13
10:32
12:30
19:26
20:18–19
23:23–26
26:48–50
28:20

Mark
5:36
11:24
12:29–31
13:7–8
14:38

Luke
6:47–49
15:1–7, 11–32
19:10
21:11

John
1:1, 12
3:16
6:35
7:37–38
9:3
10:14–15
11:25, 35, 40, 47–53
12:9–11
14:2–3, 27
15:19
16:33

Romans
1:16–17
2:6–8
5:3–4, 6–8
6:23
8:14–17, 26–27, 28,
38–39,
10:9–10
12:2
14:8, 10–12

1 Corinthians
2:9
6:19–20
13:4–7
14:33
15:33–34

2 Corinthians
1:20
3:18
4:16–18
12:10

Galatians
1:10
4:6–7
5:13, 17, 19–26

Ephesians
1:13–14
2:4–5, 8–10
4:31–32
5:4, 14
6:10–11, 12, 14–17

Philippians
4:8

Colossians
1:22
3:2

1 Timothy
6:7

2 Timothy
3:1–5, 16–17

James
1:27
2:17, 26
4:7

Hebrews
4:12, 13, 14–16
11:3
12:7, 11
13:5, 9

1 Peter
1:3–4, 6–8
5:10

2 Peter
3:7, 9, 13

1 John
1:9
3:1, 18
4:8, 19
5:11–15

3 John
1:11

Revelation
1:8
12:9
20:15
21:6–8

Made in the USA
Las Vegas, NV
25 November 2022

60290628R00061